D & F. Aldridge

Long Melford
Corpus Cristi 1975

SUFFOLK

(overleaf) *Flemings Hall, Bedingfield*

JOHN BURKE

SUFFOLK

B. T. Batsford Ltd

London

For Peter Leggett

First published 1971

© John Burke 1971

Reprinted 1973

Text printed in Great Britain by Fletcher & Son Ltd,
Norwich. Plates printed and books bound by Richard Clay
(The Chaucer Press) Ltd, Bungay, Suffolk for the publishers
B. T. Batsford Ltd, 4 Fitzhardinge Street, London W.1

ISBN 0 7134 0069 2

CONTENTS

ILLUSTRATIONS

The plates are reproduced with the kind permission of the following: Hallam Ashley: 3, 4, 9, 12, 13, 22, 34; A. F. Kersting: 5, 10, 11,
16, 17, 20, 21; The Metropolitan Museum of Art, New York, The
Cloisters Collection: 19; Louis & Daphne Peek: 7; Kenneth
Scowen: 14, 24, 27, 31; Edwin Smith: *frontispiece*, 2, 8, 15, 25, 28,
29, 30, 32, 33, 35, 37; Jeffery W. Whitelaw: 6, 18, 38, 39.

SUFFOLK

N

NORF

CAMBRIDGESHIRE

Little Ouse

Brandon
Santon Downham
Lakenheath
Elveden
Barnham
Euston
Coney Weston
Hopton
Redgrav
Barningham
Mildenhall
Honington
Icklingham
Ampton
Gt. Livermere
Walsham-le-Willows
Ingham
Ixworth
Hengrave
A45
4
Kentford
Gipping
Moulton
A45
Haugh
BURY ST. EDMUNDS
Woolpit
Stowupland
NEWMARKET
Dalham
Stowmarket
Bradfield Combust
Bradfield St Clare
Lidgate
Rede
Cockfield
3
Battisford Tye
Hartest
Thorpe Morieux
Bark
Little Bradley
Boxted
Hitcham
Bildeston
Lavenham
Chelsworth
Kedington
Cavendish
Clare
Lindsey
Haverhill
Stoke-by-Clare
Long Melford
2
Kersey
Hadle
Stour
Groton
Sudbury
Boxford
Stoke-by-Nayland
Polstead
Stratford St Mar
Bures
Nayland

ESSEX

~ARTHUR BANKS~

CHAPTER ONE

Entrances

This is a love story. It may be catalogued soberly as a work of non-fiction; but then, surely the best love stories are true?

The author of this book was neither born nor brought up in Suffolk. The author—who will henceforth call himself 'I', though using that pronoun as sparingly as possible—first came into the county many years ago up what was known in the great coaching days as the Yarmouth Road but is now prosaically labelled the A.12.

Like other invaders, I felt that at last I had found the part of the world which suited me best. Sooner or later I must make my home here. 'A county to settle down with', as William Addison truly says: 'a county to wed.' My family and I settled at last, and were made unfussily welcome. My wife does not, I think, too much resent this other protracted love affair. Nor are we too resentful of the existence of other lovers, older admirers, or even newcomers who have fallen under the same spell. We like to feel that we see and hear things which have quite escaped everyone else; and we are probably quite wrong.

Other visitors have been received less hospitably, but this has not deterred them. These others did not come deferentially across the Essex border but savagely from the sea. Wave after wave of invaders has broken on these shores throughout the centuries, often flowing far inland. Sometimes the wave ebbed. Sometimes it sank deep into the soil. One strain after another of alien blood was added to the mixture we like to think of as English, or perhaps British.

Some counties blur indistinguishably into their neighbours. From early times Suffolk has been more sharply delineated than most. The estuary and valley of the Stour in the south were reinforced by oak forests which continued their barricade round the Cambridge border to the verge of the Fens. In the north the Waveney and the Little Ouse, marking the boundary with Norfolk, can still provide an exasperating obstacle to strangers. Caught in the network of by-roads, the traveller doggedly follows a winding course like one of those tangled strands in a child's picture puzzle, hoping eventually to emerge from the maze, only to find that in real life the goal, a bridge over the water, is still miles away. Suffolk has always been virtually an island. Apart from one approach through the Devil's Dyke near Newmarket, the most obvious way in has been from the sea.

After many an influx of Rhenish, French and Belgic tribes came the Romans, who policed the Saxon shore for some 400 years. When they left in A.D. 436, the Angles from Holstein flooded greedily in and established themselves as the North Folk (Norfolk) and the South Folk (Suffolk), while the Saxons gave their names to Essex, Sussex and Wessex. In 575 East Anglia became a kingdom. Redwald was the first king to become a Christian, but his conversion was not wholehearted: the Christian altar had to take its place alongside the altars of his other gods. Shielded from neighbours by forest and water, the Angles tended to relapse into pagan ways. Devout Christians found it advisable to flee to the west.

In the ninth century the Danes began to harry the coastline and make murderous forays up creeks and inlets. In 870 they succeeded in capturing and killing the young King of East Anglia after a battle whose bloodshed reduced him to tears of horror and compassion. Unlike many of his predecessors, Edmund was an unfaltering Christian and was later canonized. Now that St George has been pronounced fictitious and England is therefore in need of an authentic patron saint, Edmund can surely claim to be first choice.

In the final stage of his martyrdom Edmund's head was cut off and for a while disappeared. Legend tells that it was guarded by a wolf until the searchers found it. The crown transfixed by arrows which appears in the county crest, and the wolf holding the saint's head between its paws in the Bury St Edmunds crest, are motifs recurring in carvings and other decorations all over the region.

The Danes were driven out of East Anglia in 920. For 70 years there was a breathing space, apart from a few scattered raids, while they turned their attention to other parts of England. Then they returned, fired Ipswich, and once more ravaged the area until the exhausted defenders agreed to pay 'protection' money in the form of Danegeld.

The last successful invasion of the country was made by the Normans on the Sussex coast. The Danes still had hopes of ultimately dominating England, and for a while their old Anglo-Saxon enemies became allies in an attempt to eject Duke William. But William was Conqueror. He strengthened his hold on the land by granting castles, manors and estates to trusted followers such as the Bigods, whose name and influence recur in Suffolk history almost as often as the name and emblem of St Edmund.

At the time of the Conquest Suffolk was, with the possible exception of Middlesex, the most densely populated part of England. Today, though thirteenth in order of size among English counties, it comes thirty-second in size of population.

It is still rich in its store of memories and treasures left by prehistoric craftsmen, by Romans, Angles, Saxons, Danes and Normans. Coins and brooches, bowls and urns of different centuries and different cultures are repeatedly disgorged from an apparently inexhaustible hoard just below the surface of the earth. Danish names and inscriptions appear in coastal villages and surprisingly far inland; Dutch architecture blends with other influences, native and imported, just as the people themselves have assimilated a mixture of influences. Martello towers defy Napoleon; crumbling concrete relics of the Second World War hump up from field and beach; overgrown runways from which planes once took off to ensure that Hitler stayed on the far side of the North Sea (referred to in the deeds of our own house as the German Ocean) are now used by learner drivers or as dumps for gas-main piping.

Everywhere are grimacing faces, ancient but vividly alive—a smug dog in a brass, a demon leering under a musty porch, strange birds mingling with angels on corbels. Some faces have had all expression obliterated or distorted by the depredations of a berserk Puritan who was almost as brutal as the Danes, though, regrettably, a son of the county.

Administratively Suffolk is divided into two sections: East Suffolk with its county town of Ipswich, and West Suffolk with its offices in Bury St Edmunds. This may make good sense in terms of local government, but for myself I visualize it in three parts, and this is loosely the pattern I have adopted for this book.

The foundation of the entire county is chalk, part of the shallow London Basin. Strips of the Crag formation which make Suffolk such a lucky dip for fossil-hunters underlie the coastal heaths, giving the area east of the A.12 markedly different characteristics from the boulder-clay loam of the west; but incongruously the seaside heathland picture is repeated on the inland rim of the county, around the chalk outcroppings of Breckland.

That there are differences in human temperament also can hardly be denied by anyone who has talked one day to a Southwold fisherman and next day to a farmer outside Stowmarket.

West of the A.12, the A.1120 runs into the A.45 to make a dividing line—part of it retracing an old Roman road—across the centre of the county to Newmarket. South of this route lies all the higher ground in Suffolk, which is admittedly not so very high: most of the county varies between 80 and 200 feet above sea level, the loftiest point being 417 feet at Rede. North of the road the landscape becomes gradually bleaker, the farms are awe-inspiringly large, and the glow of the mellow wool towns gives way to starker villages and eventually the coniferous and flinty austerity of Breckland.

Farms in East Anglia are in any case larger than in most parts of the country, some being amalgamated into groups which add up to as much as 3,000 acres. With low annual rainfall and a generally flat or mildly undulating surface, the area is especially suitable for arable crops such as potatoes, grain, and sugar beet.

Visitors often comment on the absence of sheep. Yet Suffolk rams are much sought after as a cross with other breeds, and Suffolk can be proud of establishing, as well as the Suffolk black-face, three other livestock strains of its own: Red Poll cattle, Large Black pigs,

2   *Cratfield: farmland and church*

and the Suffolk Punch horse. The sturdy Suffolk Punch was once much in demand for hauling brewers' drays and was unbeatable at heavy farm work. Now we are in the era of the tractor and the diesel lorry.

In recent decades vast numbers of trees and hedges have been felled and cut away. 'How scandalously they misuse the globe!' burst out the vicar of Bredfield to Edward Fitzgerald in the 1830s, on hearing that a local landowner proposed to fell some of his oaks. He would be appalled by our modern massacres, which open up imposing vistas to drivers and walkers but also subject them to the buffeting of unchecked winds and the blinding assault of dust or driving rain. Roads and lanes once sheltered from storm now clog up with soil, mud or snow. More serious is the long-term threat to drainage, the control of micro-organisms in the soil, and the balance of bird and animal life. Wide areas may well turn eventually into dust-bowls.

The temptations to do away with hedges are plain. Modern machinery works better over wide, uninterrupted tracts of land. A farmer paying highly for each acre of his ground wants to use every square inch and not be kept at a distance by hedges, banks and paths: an unemployable strip of a few inches all round a field adds up to an impressive area. Any landlord or farmer with a sense of responsibility to the countryside can exclude important hedges and woodlands when decreeing the removal of obstructions; but a contractor called in to do the job may suggest 'let's get rid of all the rest while we're about it', and too often a casual nod of agreement seals the fate of a hedge or copse which is not merely pleasing to the eye but of great importance to the whole ecological structure.

In recent years efforts have been made to halt the destruction. Since 1959 the Conservation Corps has deployed volunteer labour, particularly at weekends and during holiday periods, to maintain nature reserves, clear neglected paths, replant trees and hedges, build dams and protect ponds, fens and heaths. Many fine principles were proclaimed during Conservation Year, 1970. Their implementation should not be left to a dedicated handful of people struggling to help the community in spite of itself.

Mercifully, quite apart from restoration and conservation work

3-6 *Wind and water mills: 3 Herringfleet; 4 Baylham; 5 Buttram's, Woodbridge; 6 Saxtead Green*

now in hand, there are still many original hedgerows left, in winter darkly spiked against the steely sky, later vibrant with primroses, poppies, cowslips and violets. In spite of winds blustering from the sea or scouring dry topsoil from the land, wild flowers and garden flowers flourish in a profusion which is all part of the East Anglian exuberance. 'If you can stand it for six months', newcomers are told, 'you'll live for ever.' The most unlikely plant immigrants, once rooted, decide to show what they, too, can do. As long as there is something growing somewhere, anywhere, a local church is bound to stage a flower festival. By the roadside many a lovingly tended array of antirrhinums, wallflowers and aubretia is banked away from the house as though the occupants wished others to have the pleasure of seeing what they themselves cannot see from their own windows. Showing off, perhaps? But the owners have reason for pride, and do provide delight for the passer-by.

Between the remaining banks and coppices many lanes are, in spite of the generally unrumpled landscape, as convoluted as mountain passes. Even though St Christopher has been sent to join St George in the limbo of those who never really existed, you may wish to play safe by offering up a quiet prayer for your preservation from the sudden appearance of combine harvesters, ploughs or mechanical hedge-trimmers on the road ahead of you. Even a school bus can be a major hazard.

Nor are the trees all gone yet. Great avenues of elms swallow you up, spruce and fir and lime close in, beech and chestnut link fingers overhead, until a sudden upthrust of the road like a launching ramp threatens to spill you out of this shadowy magical world into the vast sky.

The sky ... or, rather, the skies. No book can set out to chart the loveliest aspect of Suffolk and indeed of all East Anglia. Landscape may be described with reasonable fidelity and its contours will remain reasonably the same between the time these chapters are written and the time they are read. But how can one write a gazetteer of the heavens? They are never the same two days running: rarely consistent any two hours running. These dizzying skies, like no other skies in the world, intoxicated Constable and drive lesser painters to distraction. They dominate the county and overawe the human figures moving across it. You must come to see for yourself; and here, at least, you may be sure that what you see will each time be gratifyingly different from what anyone else has ever seen.

CHAPTER TWO

The Stour and the
Wool Towns

The dual carriageway racing across the Essex border towards Ipswich cuts off the village of Stratford St Mary from its church, now isolated on a mound which seems to belong rather to nearby Dedham. Abandoned by through traffic, the street that was once a main road has sunk into an agreeable sleepiness to which the steady mumble of the overriding A.12 is only a somnolent accompaniment. The atmosphere is spoilt only by a pallid box of a building looking like a cross between an atomic power station and some dictator's mausoleum, which is in fact a pumping station for Southend waterworks.

Old-fashioned signposts have gone. On the A.12 great shimmering plaques warn you well in advance where you must be prepared to turn off for those little towns and villages so close to the wide swathe of road yet so remote from it. The names, at any rate, are unchanged and as alluring as ever.

It is hard to know which to resist, which to choose. Ahead lies the sprawl of Ipswich. Try that first and you may well decide to turn back and give Suffolk a miss altogether. Plunge too abruptly into the ruminating valley of the Stour and you could succumb too rapturously to its enchantments and wish to go neither forward nor back.

For an attractive compromise, why not start with Hadleigh?

Approached from Holton St Mary, the long, radiant street into the town offers a preview of most Suffolk building styles and colours: washes of Suffolk pink, ochre, green and yellow; brick, pargeting, and timber. At a T-junction the road from Ipswich to Sudbury feeds in and spurs one to rush through with no more than a vaguely approving glance at a flicker of Georgian frontages, off-white brick, and golden stonecrop bubbling out of darkened roof tiles. The kaleidoscope is charming, but to hurry through in such a manner is to miss all that Hadleigh has to offer.

Pargeting can be regarded as a regional delicacy. These designs on house façades were originally raised from or indented into plasterwork with a kind of comb or, later, a trowel. The finished patterns varied in style and sophistication. Earliest examples used simple representation of ropes and birds' feet, supplemented by more or less inventive flourishes of dots. Local craftsmen developed personal techniques and embellishments, some naïve and some quite ambitious, each carrying an implicit trademark as distinctive as a thatcher's. Even modern building estates try to preserve continuity with the past by introducing squared-up panels of diagonal tracings or other fairly straightforward ornamentation. The simple reliefs on one frontage in Hadleigh High Street have been brightly painted and are accompanied by an unexpected clock face.

The church square, rich in summer with the heady aroma of honeysuckle, is warmed by the glowing red brick of the deanery tower and the curry-coloured wash of plaster and timber on the Guildhall. The tower was built by Archdeacon Pykenham in 1495 as part of his palace, and restored in 1961 when the imitation Tudor deanery of the early nineteenth century had to be demolished. Here in 1833 was the virtual beginning of the Oxford Movement, when Dean Rose, then rector, convened a meeting of fellow thinkers who, during the conference, conceived the influential *Tracts for the Times*. The Guildhall, or Cloth Hall, was the meeting place of five major guilds and is a reminder of the weavers' prosperity throughout the Middle Ages and up to the first half of the seventeenth century. We are on the fringe (an appropriate enough word) of the rich wool country.

The church itself supports a soaring lead spire on a wooden framework which throws the building and its square somehow out of proportion; yet this same spire is most inviting when seen from a distance as one descends into the town. Within, a bench end depicts

the head of St Edmund not between the paws but in the jaws of his
guardian wolf, which seems oddly to be wearing shoes and an ecclesiastical collar. King Guthrum, the Christianized Dane to whom
Alfred conceded the monarchy of East Anglia, is reputed to be buried
beneath the present church, though the tomb canopy in the south
aisle know as Guthrum's Tomb is manifestly five centuries too late.

Near the font is a capacious eighteenth-century gotch, or beer
mug, for the benefit of the bellringers.

Overall House in High Street preserves the memory of John Overall, who with John Bloise of nearby Nettlestead played a large part in
the translation of the Bible into the Authorized Version of 1611.
Overall later became Bishop of Lichfield and then of Norwich. The
existing font is that in which he was baptized in 1559, a cover being
dedicated to him by the Archbishop of Canterbury in 1925.

The gentle hill out of Hadleigh towards Ipswich boasts some
sagging but picturesque houses, propped up by recent additions. The
old people's home a few yards up the slope is attractively laid out,
but it is rather unfortunate that it should be called Angel Court:
elderly the inhabitants may be, but in such delightful surroundings
they are surely in no hurry to move on.

This was the direction taken by Rowland Taylor on his way to
death at the stake. A Catholic converted to Protestantism, he became
Cranmer's chaplain and rector of Hadleigh. When Bloody Mary's
persecutions reached the town, he was arrested because of his
attempt to prevent the celebration by an intrusive priest of Mass in
his church, and condemned to death. Led by night through the town
to Aldham Common, he declared: 'Thanked be God, I am even at
home.' A memorial now stands on the spot where he was burnt to
death.

Further along the Ipswich road is Hintlesham Hall, the home of
other religious dissidents. Built by the recusant Timperley in the
time of Elizabeth I, it has a ceiling bearing the initials of a later
Timperley who also had ideas of his own and was compelled to leave
the country because of his support for James II. Its annual music
festival, less ambitious and more intimate than that of Aldeburgh,
now seems well-established.

7 *Flatford: Willy Lott's cottage*

Havelock Ellis spent his declining years and died in Hintlesham. His views on *Sex in Relation to Society* or, indeed, on sex in relation to anything whatsoever scandalized his contemporaries but would cause little more than a snigger from our own contemporaries, who do not realize how hard he worked for a freedom that is now in danger of being casually misused.

Too far along this road and you will be sucked in by Ipswich as surely as if you had stayed on the A.12. Beter, in spite of its dangerous enchantments, to turn back and risk the Stour Valley.

'Constable country' has become a hackneyed phrase by now but cannot be shrugged off. Born at East Bergholt on 11 June 1776, John Constable made the river and its environs his own and has imposed his vision of them upon us for all time. The son of a prosperous miller who wanted the boy to follow the family tradition, he determined to become a painter. 'A natural painter', he insisted, defying both classicism and the current fashion for the supposedly sublime and picturesque. The river walks, the trees, shadows, sun and cloud shaped his affections and his talents. 'The sound of water escaping from mill-dams, willows, slimy posts and brickwork—I love such things.' Even when he was far away, living another life and painting other scenes, he never really escaped: 'Painting with me is another word for feeling, and I associate my careless boyhood with all that lies on the banks of the Stour; those scenes made me a painter.'

Flatford Mill is still there, now in the hands of the National Trust. Willy Lott's cottage has been preserved, charming yet less real than its substantial ghost on canvas. The river meanders between the same banks overhung by willows which we all knew before ever visiting this part of the world. Banks and trees may have been attacked by a salt intake during this century, and there may be a rash of tea-shops and car-parks, but this is still the country which belongs to John Constable rather than he to it.

The great Perpendicular tower dominating the countryside, forever associated in paint with an attendant rainbow, is that of Stoke-by-Nayland. The village must always have been too small for its massive church, and today seems utterly inadequate. The half-timbered cottages beside the church, so often photographed for

olde-worlde calendars, are in reality scarred and despondent. Once
lost, they cannot be restored. Gifford's Hall and the gabled and
plastered seventeenth-century Thorington Hall survive. Tendring
Hall is gone. Taking its name from Tendring in Essex, it was a home
of the Howards until 1563, when their estates were forfeited. In
the church remains a brass of Lady Catherine Howard, two of whose
great-granddaughters, her namesake and Anne Boleyn, were among
the wives of Henry VIII.

Among many evocative entries in the parish register is the
following:

For two men to watch all night with a man	1s	8d
For releife in the morning		6d
Hue and cry to Polstead		5d
Charges for a man in the stocks	1s	0d
For carrying a person to Bury gaol	1s	10d

The name of Polstead strikes a chord. The melodrama of Maria
Marten's murder in the Red Barn is linked in my mind with Sweeney
Todd and the touring performances of Tod Slaughter in what might
nowadays be advertised as a Double Horror Bill. It was startling to
learn in due course that the story was true. There really was a Maria
Marten, a village girl infatuated with William Corder, the local
ne'er-do-well, though it is doubtful whether she was quite the inno-
cent maiden portrayed on stage. Believing that they were running
away to be married, she met Corder late one night in the Red Barn
and there was murdered. After a hideously repetitive dream her
mother insisted that the floor of the barn should be dug up, and there
the corpse was found. Corder was tried and hanged.

The Red Barn has since burned down, but Maria's cottage still
stands, and her gravestone was once to be found in the churchyard:
it was, indeed, found too frequently by souvenir hunters, who
chipped away so many fragments that it has now been replaced by
a starkly matter-of-fact varnished noticeboard. Some remains of
Corder may also be seen, but not here. His scalp and a book bound
in his skin, together with two pistols and a knife which may have

been the murder weapon, are preserved in Moyse's Hall Museum, Bury St Edmunds.

Polstead today would be glad to forget this grisly association. Sprinkled in handfuls on and below a huddle of low hills, it exudes an air of leisure and good fellowship from its fine old houses, with some good conversions and pleasant if unremarkable modern villas perched around and between snug cottages with disciplined gardens. In 1967 and 1969 the R.D.C. commended it as the best-kept village in the area, and clearly no inhabitant will be permitted to let the side down.

On an eminence above the duckpond, church and hall look out across the valley to the mightier hulk of Stoke-by-Nayland breasting the skyline. Polstead church holds a mystery of its own. The nave arcades and windows contain brickwork dating from Norman times. Yet during this period there was almost no brick-making in England. After the departure of the Romans, their successors made use of bricks which had been left behind but apparently forgot how to make any for themselves, even in East Anglia with its abundance of suitable clay. Perhaps in Polstead one little group retained some skill and strove to keep the craft alive.

The thirteenth-century font was restored in 1961 and provided in 1964 with a fibreglass cover, its wavy surface representing the waters of baptism and carrying replicas of three primitive New Testament scenes. This was designed and executed by a member of the Community of St Clare who was trained at the Slade before taking up her vocation as a nun.

Along the Stour we follow a course which has been travelled by barge, train, and now by lorries and cars. These were the towpaths along which horses trod, pulling barges behind them until the iron horses drove them out of business. Now the old Stour Valley railway line is itself as overgrown and choked with nostalgia as paths and river bank.

Each change provokes mourners. The horse-lover would be amazed to know that his successors grow sentimental over noisy, noisome steam engines. We all want things as *we* have seen and known them: an ugly Victorian house, derided by architectural purists, was the scene of youthful happiness and ought not to be replaced by a block of flats; a clock, absurdly anachronistic in an ancient tower, has been there since our childhood and therefore belongs. The world sets in a certain mould at one ideal moment for each one of us: what happened before was merely a leading-up to this perfection, and any later alteration is for the worse. 'I should like everyone to go about doing just as he pleased,' said Max Beerbohm tolerantly, 'short of altering any of the things to which I have grown accustomed.'

Nayland is another deferential cluster below a declamatory church tower, this one with a spire. The original flint tower had just such a spire, but when this became unstable in the 1830s it was replaced by a brick superstructure. In 1884 the tower was jarred by an earth tremor which shook Essex and this part of Suffolk, and although it survived precariously until 1963, complete overhaul then became necessary. During this restoration a replica of the original spire was set upon the tower.

Within St James' are a splendid roof, a font cover designed by the creator of the Lion and the Unicorn pavilion in the Festival of Britain, and a recently repainted eighteenth-century gallery and renovated organ. There is also one of Constable's only two sacred paintings, of historical rather than aesthetic interest. From a rood screen taken down in the nineteenth century, eight painted panels have survived, including the inevitable St Edmund. A zealous caretaker disapproved of their murky surface and gave them a good scrubbing with harsh soap and water. The salvaged remains have now been cleaned and hardened as well as possible and are to be found on the wall of the south aisle.

It is not far from here to Bures, whose tower also once bore a spire. It is claimed that St Edmund was crowned here on Christmas Day 855, but most authorities now accept that the ceremony was actually performed on a hill outside the town—not, to add further confusion, on the so-called St Edmund's Hill but beside the Bures to Boxford road. On this spot Stephen Langton later consecrated a chapel, used as a barn until recent times but now refurbished with glass and monuments from Colne Priory in Essex.

The border with Essex here takes a steep turn to the north.

Enclosed in this arm, a few miles 'inland', as it were, from the Stour are the wool towns which gave Suffolk its most prosperous years and also its most magnificent churches, erected or at the very least provided with solid financial foundation by rich weavers who, having stored up profit in this world, were beginning to have doubts about their dividends in the next.

Spinning and weaving for home wear went on in most parts of England, but there was soon a much more widespread demand for Suffolk specialities, particularly dyed cloth. Woollen cloth was on sale in Bury market before the end of the twelfth century and probably also at fairs, when London merchants were among the most important customers. A leading cloth manufacturer in London in 1296 was a Fulk de St Edmunds. At Hadleigh a poll tax return from the late fourteenth century shows that one in five of the male population was employed in the industry. Anyone with money to invest set himself up with clothier's equipment. Looms, tenters for drying and stretching cloth on tenterhooks, and the apparatus for fulling and dyeing were all packed into cottage rooms or, when income justified it, into specially constructed manufactories.

Among the emblems to be found on pargeting in this area are various guild insignia, including that of St Blaise, adopted as patron saint of the wool trade because he was said to have been combed to death during the Diocletian persecution.

Boxford did well from the wool industry over a period of 300 years. A memorial in St Mary's church reads: 'Here lyeth interred the body of William Cobbold Clothier.' It is one of many in this and other local churches which could lead us vaguely to suppose that 'Clothier' was the surname of a prolific local family. A pity that the choir stalls and the low dais in the children's corner should clumsily and unnecessarily obscure several of the finely lettered slabs.

The wooden porch may possibly be the oldest in the country.

This is a district of which a cheerful but shrewd resident once said to me: 'Local politics are so fierce round here—all the societies and groups, the sewing circles, clubs and so on—you daren't have a holiday. Go away for three days, and by the time you get back there's been a *coup d'état.*' It might disconcert the outsider, but it's great fun for the participants.

Boxford takes its name simply enough from a ford over the Box. Another local village, standing on both sides of a tributary of the Brett, was known long ago as Carseye, 'Car' being the old name for a stream and 'Seye' meaning a ditch. This has now become Kersey, with the stream running across the lowest dip of the street, and ducks taking precedence over wheeled traffic.

Kersey is very nearly too good to be true. It is best seen on a bright spring day, before the summer coaches roll through and the cameras snap or whirr from both steep pavements. Not that one can blame a photographer for wishing to capture this lovely street. Looked down on from either end, from the steps below the church or from the corner that turns breathtakingly in from the north, it offers itself as that unspoilt haven to which all of us feel we would one day wish to retire. Are those timbered cottages, those brightly washed walls, plunging towards the footbridge over the watersplash, too pretty: is the whole village—'the most picturesque in South Suffolk', according to Pevsner—too much an artificially preserved daydream? I think not. Prettiness is not to be despised; loving care not to be condemned as self-indulgence.

The original church, probably a small thatched building, is mentioned in Domesday Book. The later edifice suffered badly during the Reformation and then again during Victorian times. The flint tower has weathered five centuries but in recent times has been found in need of repair.

In 1964, warned that the bells which had last pealed at the time of Queen Victoria's Jubilee were in a dangerous condition, the village set to work. It staged a flower festival in 1965, repeated annually, and solicited contributions into a tin standing in the watersplash. From £350 in the first year to £750 in 1969, devoted workers raised over £3,000 to set things right. Unfortunately, while this was going on it was discovered that the tower itself was in no condition to carry the peal. At least £12,000 would be required to strengthen it, and still more expenditure was called for in the body of the church. All this from a village of 300 people!

Kersey is not an isolated case. Everywhere noble buildings are decaying, threatening to collapse, demanding more money for surgery and healing than can possibly be granted. In one small town the lord of the manor gave the proceeds from a traction engine rally to his local church. Surveying the churned-up morass afterwards, he decided it had been worth it: 'Look at it this way—it was the equivalent of 200 years of church fêtes.' In too many places the bazaars and fêtes and jumble sales provide too little, too late.

The tin remains in Kersey watersplash to collect donations. A sponsored walk led by the novelist Hammond Innes and his wife covered 20 miles and raised over £700. Direct appeals have been made to trusts and charities, and many visitors and anonymous donors who wished there to be no flaw in the picture of the village which they retained in their minds sent money. The appeal fund has still a long way to go; but the bells have been installed in their new frame and, after testing, were rung at a dedication service on 5 June 1970.

Having taken its name from the stream, Kersey passed it on to a cloth woven here for men's apparel, while nearby Lindsey wove a lighter material for women which came to be known as Lindsey Woolsey.

St James' Chapel in Lindsey, classified as an Ancient Monument, is a curiosity, a domestic 'free' chapel independent of the parish priest and archdeacon, and possibly attached to the castle of which only a few lumpy vestiges remain. The freedom was abolished in 1547, and the building was used as a barn until 1930. St Peter's is a true village church, stark and simple and somehow domesticated. It has an ancient font, a few traces of wall painting, box pews, decaying woodwork; and has the feeling of belonging to the community, of being alive rather than merely preserved.

Although a near neighbour, the parish of Groton has none of the same character and compactness. It consists of a scattering of hamlets with gay names like Daisy Green and Gosling Green, its main claim to fame being as the manor granted by Henry VIII to a wealthy clothier from Lavenham, Adam Winthrop. Adam's grandson chose to leave Groton and encouraged others to accompany him: he went to the New World, became first Governor of Massachusetts, and founded the city of Boston.

Kersey has a beautiful rival not too far away. Downhill past the trees of Chelsworth Hall we negotiate a double-humped switchback bridge and find ourselves in a village street offering an unspoilt spread of timber, thatch and trim gardens. Windows are gay with pot plants and bowls of flowers. Somewhere a goose cackles, a cock crows, and above the stillness of the pond is a mutter of pigeons. Chelsworth was the place which Julian Tennyson, writing just before the Second World War, loved above all others. He was killed in that war. It would be good to know that in some private heaven he is allowed to saunter every morning along that tranquil street and chat to people of like mind.

Here, too, the church has its problems. Money for its repair and upkeep is raised each year on a summer Sunday when as many as possible of the village gardens are opened to the public, who pay an inclusive charge and are free to wander where they like.

The route now leads inevitably through Monks Eleigh, foaming with roses and geraniums in the warm months, to Lavenham.

Lavenham arouses the same instinctive mistrust (soon overcome) as Kersey. The splendid marketplace looks like a film set. It was in fact used as such, with little need to conceal any of its existing features, in Michael Reeves' chilling horror film, *Witchfinder General*. Lest it be supposed, having moved so swiftly from the story of Maria Marten to one of witchcraft, that Suffolk has an inclination towards the macabre, I hasten to add that in Shilling Old Grange, Shilling Street, Jane Taylor wrote *Twinkle, twinkle, little star*. Another house in the town also claims this privilege, but although it is true that Jane lived there on returning to Lavenham after some years' absence, it was certainly not her home when she penned the immortal lines. The 'Shilling', incidentally, has nothing to do with money: it is a corruption of Schylling, the name of one of the Flemings who came here in great numbers during the fourteenth and fifteenth centuries.

Lavenham must have existed in Roman times, as coins of many Emperors have been ploughed up, along with various urns, graves

9 *Lavenham: fifteenth-century Wool Hall (incorporated in Swan Hotel, 1963)*

and ovens. It was important enough to be included in Domesday Book.

Among the oldest existing buildings are the weavers' cottages in Water Street, in a decrepit state at the end of the last war but now well restored. Here and elsewhere through the town settled Flemish immigrants. Like many immigrants before and since, they added to the country's resources and skills, but were not automatically loved for it. One Robert Tavell of Lavenham, who took part in the Peasant Rising of 1381, seems to have been an early racialist: his pet hate was Flemings, and he did all he could to drive them out. But they and their looms were here to stay.

One of the finest half-timbered buildings in England is the Guild-hall, where clothiers came to argue wages and prices, settle disputes, and generally organize their profession. An important member of the fraternity was Thomas Spring, a Durham cloth merchant whose son Thomas also prospered in this field. And there was another Thomas yet to come.

After the victory at Bosworth, the second Thomas Spring was persuaded by John de Vere, Earl of Oxford, to collaborate on the building of a church tower in thanksgiving. He lived to see the foundations of the tower laid but died in 1486, leaving a large sum towards further work. His son, the third Thomas Spring, found it easy to carry out these wishes, since he was even more successful in business than his father or grandfather and was dubbed Thomas Spring the Rich Clothier. There is some suspicion that his riches were not won quite as honestly as might have been wished of a devout churchgoer, the guiding spirit behind the completion of Lavenham's pride. At one stage he had to ask the King for a pardon, granted readily enough (since he was a splendid source of income from taxation), for 'all usurious contracts, usurious bargains, corrupt covenants, of illicit sales of cloth, wool, linen, and for non-payment of foreign merchants, for all false deception and offences in making cloth, in stretching out the length, or the breadth of it, and all deception in the selling of woollen cloth'. The rich clothier would not, one feels, have looked kindly on modern inventions such as the Trade Descriptions Act.

10 *Lavenham: SS Peter and Paul*
11 *Long Melford: Holy Trinity*

Whatever his transgressions, this third Thomas continued to be respected. By the time the tower and chapel of the church were completed, the Springs had been granted a coat of arms, which appears 32 times round the top of the tower. It has been said that the tower is too massive for the main body of the church, which Pugin declared to be the finest example of Late Perpendicular in the world; but once it has imposed itself on the vision it is impossible to imagine the building any other way. The porch was a gift of that John de Vere who started the whole project. Two boars in the spandrel form a 'pun in stone' on the family name, 'verres' being Latin for a boar.

Thomas Spring the Rich Clothier left it in his will that his body should be buried in the church before the altar of St Catherine. In view of his contribution towards the building, there was no argument about this. He and his wife Alice lie behind a splendid wooden screen or parclose, probably executed by Flemish craftsmen, and in addition to the figure of St Catherine we find, not surprisingly, that of St Blaise.

Celebration of the church's completion in 1525 was unfortunately disrupted by outbreaks of rioting against taxes levied, complained the hard-pressed workers and merchants, to support Henry VIII's war in France. In *Henry* VIII, Act I, Shakespeare has the Duke of Norfolk plead the rioters' cause before the King and Cardinal Wolsey, himself of Suffolk origin:

> The clothiers all, not able to maintain
> Them any to them 'longing, have put off
> The spinsters, carders, fullers, weavers, who
> Unfit for other life, compelled by hunger
> And lack of other means, in desperate manner
> Daring the event to the teeth, are all in uproar . . .

The conversation in many a Suffolk house and street today runs often on similar topics. Then, as now, the grumblers found it possible to go on living and working in spite of fresh demands on their pockets. Lavenham's prosperity continued until, like its neighbours, it began to suffer from the invention of fulling machines worked by water instead of by foot, which caused a trade drift towards the west. In addition, silk was becoming more fashionable. At one stage Queen Elizabeth tried to succour the wool trade by enacting that her subjects should be buried in woollen shrouds. But royal or parliamentary decrees cannot renew the life of something which is due for extinction. When we speak of the Industrial Revolution we think of a later century. There is, however, nothing new in industrial revolutions. From the day when the first spark was struck or the first wheel turned there has been constant need for heartbreaking readjustments and reassessments.

Trade declined, and Lavenham lost its importance. The merchant princes faded away. The Guildhall, once the hub of so much activity, became a prison, kept in such bad repair that inmates were known to kick their way out through the plaster walls. Those who remained within did not have to sew mailbags, a later chore: as local felons they spent their time on the only trade which, though ailing, the local folk knew—spinning wool. Later the hall became a workhouse and an almshouse. It passed eventually into the hands of the Quilter family and in this century was presented to the National Trust.

The Wool Hall, built during the fifteenth century by the Guild of Our Lady for use as an Exchange, also lost its *raison d'être*. It was divided into houses and a shop, and then in 1911 was sold and dismantled into numbered segments, to be added to a cottage owned by Princess Louise near Ascot. At the last moment such a fuss was raised that the Princess generously agreed to return the timbers to Lavenham so that the hall could be restored to its original position. It then became a home for women railway workers. Now it has been incorporated into the 'Swan' hotel.

The 'Swan' has grown steadily since the war, swallowing adjoining buildings and laying out a modern car park and ambitious gardens. Most of the work has been done with discretion, using the different levels to give a sense of leisurely informality. During the war it was a haunt of servicemen, including Americans from nearby air bases. They etched their names all over the bar, and these signatures are now preserved behind a glass panel on the wall.

It is rather a pity, though, that the lounge formed from the salvaged Wool Hall should now resonate to the boom of a television set.

From here it is only a few miles into Sudbury, the 'Eatanswill' of *Pickwick Papers*. Defoe said of it: 'I know nothing for which this town is remarkable, except for being very populous and very poor.' Sudbury has been populous over many centuries and often very poor, suffering from fluctuations in its fortunes as a wool town, a market town and, in the early nineteenth century, a silk weaving town. Today we know a bit more than Defoe: since his time, the naming of Gainsborough Street commemorates Sudbury's most remarkable son.

The house in which Thomas Gainsborough was born in 1727 was originally Tudor, but the Georgian front is believed to have been added by the painter's father a few years before Thomas' birth. (Other experts declare with equal assurance that it was added some years after the birth.) Thomas went to a school run by his uncle, and then in his early teens was apprenticed to a London engraver. At the age of 19 he met and married Margaret Burr, who had a fair-sized private income, most useful for a struggling young painter. They settled into a house in Friars Street, part of the Georgian group still standing there today, and Thomas set up in business as a portrait painter, rather as a young photographer might set up shop today in the hope of making a living from wedding pictures, family groups, and beaming babies. Two daughters, whose pictures their father was so often to paint, were born here before the Gainsboroughs moved to Ipswich.

Thomas painted many landscapes, and Constable said of him: 'I fancy I see Gainsborough under every hedge and hollow tree.' Yet much of his supposedly outdoor work was done indoors. Instead of working from life he often used and re-used models made by himself from wood and plaster. In many paintings appears and reappears a plaster horse to which he resorted when other inspiration failed him. This model has been lent by Colonel Constable, a descendant of that other Stour Valley painter, to the museum which is now in the old family home in Gainsborough Street, with a simple but

12   *Ickworth House (1794-1830): the Pompeian room*

attractive garden behind it. In 1968 Rowland Suddaby was appointed curator. His own watercolours of East Anglia display a fascination with the conflict between land and sky which is—dare one say it?—closer to the obsessions of Constable than the cooler ratiocinations of Gainsborough.

In Sudbury the off-white brick which punctuates the frontages of Hadleigh comes into its own. After the gay plasters of so many villages of the region, this prevailing greyness gives a rather chill overall impression. If Sudbury appeals, it is in its proportions rather than its colouring.

Here as in so many market towns there is a sharp distinction between early closing day, when everybody seems to have sunk into a trance as deep as that following Christmas dinner or to have gone disloyally shopping in Colchester, and market day or Saturday morning, when it is unsafe to loiter and study the architecture and above all to step off the pavement for a better view of an interesting upper storey, of which Sudbury has many.

We came in from Lavenham. Leaving, we find to the south a choice between Essex and the Stour back towards Bures. North-west by north lies Long Melford, and slightly to the north-east is Acton, worth a brief visit simply for a glimpse of the life-size military brass of Sir Robert de Bures, who died in 1302. This is the oldest remaining brass in Suffolk and the third oldest in England. Other worthwhile brasses not too distant are in Little Waldingfield and Long Melford.

Melford is indeed long. Its main street is also wide, flanked by houses and shops in a medley of styles which produce harmony rather than discord. Obviously it has been here for some considerable time. Coins and burial remains from the Romano-British era have been found all round the village, and in 1958 sewage excavations uncovered a fine tessellated pavement and fragments of a bath from what must have been a Roman villa of some size.

In the twelfth century the Melford manor of the Abbot of St Edmundsbury was embedded in a luxuriantly wooded deer park of ancient foundation. At no time was there a royal hunting forest within the boundaries of Suffolk, so it escaped the restrictions of forest law. Certain demands were nevertheless made on the district

13 Woolpit: village green and nineteenth-century tower of fifteenth-century St Mary's

from time to time. When the great abbey was in the charge of Abbot Samson towards the end of that century he was asked by his superior, the Bishop of Ely, for timber which could be used in the construction of a great manor for the bishop. Reluctantly the abbot had to grant the request, whereupon one of the bishop's household arrived with the specification that the timber should be taken from Elmswell. Samson was immensely cheered by this. Undoubtedly the bishop had meant to choose timber from Elmsett rather than from Elmswell, where there was little worth having. In fact the bishop had already sent a carpenter in secret to mark the Elmsett trees of highest calibre. Having confirmed acceptance of the bishop's requirements, Abbot Samson had the surreptitiously marked trees at Elmsett felled, along with another hundred of his own choice, and hastily added them to the material already accumulated for the tower and other parts of St Edmunds itself. When the bishop realized his mistake he sent a messenger to say that he had meant Elmsett all along, not Elmswell. Abbot Samson could only report that all available wood had been set aside for the abbey and that, much as it pained him, he was unable to help the bishop.

As though the spacious street with its fine eating and drinking establishments were not enough, at the end of the village a gentle ascent, concealed until one is past the hospitable 'Bull' hotel, reveals further beauty. The sloping green is as ample as the street in its dimensions. Its large triangle has many diminutive echoes all over the county. A similar pattern will be found in more villages than one can name: a slanting green, often with a rustic shelter or abandoned pump in the middle. is flanked on one side by a through road and on the other by a narrower street which may wind its way out behind a row of plastered cottages with sagging oversailing (one cottage usually housing the post office and general store) or finish up in a cul-de-sac. The base of the triangle tends to be higher than the apex, and behind its row of cottages will be the church. From Long Melford both forking roads have outlets. To one side the main road leads on to Bury St Edmunds, overlooked by the rich red brick mansion of Melford Hall. Built at the beginning of Elizabeth I's reign and sporting flamboyant turrets above its high wall, the hall is open on certain weekdays during the summer. The other fork cuts a swathe through the green and curves to the contour of the Stour. A spur leads up to the crown of the hill and the church of Holy Trinity.

The full length of the church is not appreciated until one has cleared the Scylla and Charybdis of the Elizabethan almshouses re-fashioned by the Victorians and now a hospital, and the row of pleasant cottages culminating in an eyesore which was once a Dr Barnardo's home. Holy Trinity deserves a book to itself. It is impossible to find an architect, artist or writer who does not regard it as the finest example of this, that, or the other. It is equally impossible to stand below where it lies like an exquisite ship along the ridge and not agree that here is one of the loveliest sights in the county. It has grandeur without pomposity, style without affectation, and a lightness which implies that it rose spontaneously from the earth instead of having to be put laboriously together, stone by stone.

These stones are virtual gems. They present the finest example (let us fall into line with all the other panegyricists) of another Suffolk speciality, flushwork. This involves the blending of flint and freestone into designs which are structurally sound as well as visually satisfying. Flint has been plentiful here since prehistoric times and has been used with matter-of-fact liberality; but has also been used by craftsmen who have tamed its harshness. Most Suffolk churches have at least a little chessboard corner of flushwork some-where. Woodbridge has a richly adorned porch; Southwold makes sparing but effective use of panels; Blaxhall's flint has been integra-ted with brick. At Melford the flushwork is as lavish and yet as disciplined as a Bach fugue—the whole *Art of Fugue*, even. The face of the church dominating hill and village is flawless. It seems rather shameful that the north side should, with the exception of the clerestory, be so much plainer, like the stained and grubby back of a stage set on which it has been decided to economize. Presumably it was felt that few would ever stroll round to this part of the church-yard, and without a telescope the inhabitants of Kentwell Hall, far across the parkland at the end of a noble avenue of limes, would be unlikely to notice the deficiency.

The original tower was struck by lightning, shored up with brick-work and later with cement inserts, until in 1903 it was given its present appearance.

The church is lucky in the quantity and quality of its fifteenth-century stained glass, including a rare Lily Crucifixion, in which the lily of Mary's annunciation carries like stigmata the premonition of Christ's death on the Cross. The Lady Chapel, restored with cool elegance, has a fine carved roof. Marked out on the east wall is a multiplication table dating from the seventeenth century, when the chapel was used as a schoolroom.

For all its individual treasures, the interior leaves an oddly un-satisfactory aftertaste. The whole is not a whole. Yet I defy anyone to walk away down the path towards the village and not stop to look back, and look back ... and look back just once more.

The road to Cavendish resumes that saunter along the valley of the meditative Stour. The water meadows are perhaps not quite as lush as those between Flatford and Nayland, but they are just as enervating : there is no hurry, no reason for going on, no real urge to go anywhere else at all.

In 1960 Cavendish sported the trophy for 'the best-kept village in Suffolk' and erected a sign on the green to commemorate it. The green has the proportions of many a small city park or playground, sloping up from the arc of the main road towards a fine L-formation of fourteenth-century thatched and plastered cottages. These cottages were in a sorry condition in 1956 but were saved and restored, and now threaten to oust Kersey as the most-photographed scene in Suffolk. Behind them, the church tower is topped by a bellcote above the stair turret. Two new houses on the western edge of the green help rather than detract from its symmetry.

A pair of Restoration cottages have been combined into the 'Grape Vine', one of the rare good restaurants in an area not noted for its gastronomic pleasures. Its exterior has oblong panels of straight-forward pargeting and one great square of more ambitious reliefs. The old rectory now houses Sue Ryder's home for refugees. In 1381 a son of the Chief Justice, Sir John Cavendish, was among those of the King's attendants who fell on Wat Tyler and stabbed him after the Lord Mayor had struck him to the ground at Smithfield. Some of Tyler's enraged followers sought out Sir John, who hid his valuables in the Cavendish belfry and ran for his life, only to be trapped near Lakenheath and beheaded.

The 'Railway Arms' stands above a level crossing whose gates will not be required to open for any more trains. Beyond the bridge into Essex is a raised footwalk above the level of the frequent flood-waters.

A few minutes along the A.1092, and we are in Clare, taking its name from the family whose male line was extinguished at the battle of Bannockburn. A surviving sister, Elizabeth de Burgh, founded Clare College, Cambridge. The town was of some consequence during the thirteenth century and still has the air of a town rather than a village, though its population is only some 1,300.

The priest's house at a corner of the churchyard has a fine gable, a window with carved arms, and great swirls of heavy pargeting, including the date 1473. The 'Swan' inn has an interesting swan and foliage bracket. Branching from the middle of the main thorough-fare is the B.1063, from which Bridewell Street leads to Upper Common and the site of Clare Camp, identified by some as an Iron Age fort and by others as a Danish earthwork. It is a rectangular enclosure of about seven acres, surrounded by a double bank and ditch. Two sides have been encroached on by houses, to some extent masking the original shape.

The remains of the castle, dating from Norman times, consist now only of a shattered keep with three buttresses thrusting up like a vast splintered tooth from trees which are themselves choked by rapacious ivy. Part of the bailey was commandeered for the railway station, itself now on its way to becoming an abandoned ancient monument.

In the thirteenth century the Clare family established the Austin friars in their first English priory. A moat was dug round the grounds and still survives as the so-called 'old river'. In the early sixteenth century the priory was dissolved as a religious foundation and transferred to a Richard Frende who was to describe himself in his will as

47

'trumpeter to King Edward VI'. He converted most of the buildings to domestic use or into barns and outhouses.

A mantelpiece carved by a Cambridge craftsman at the beginning of this century embodies incidents from 'The Legend of Clare'. Sceptics will not unreasonably regard this ghost story as pure fiction, and like most stories of its kind it has acquired additional embroidery while passing from one narrator to another. Many details of the original narrative did not fit in with the layout of the priory as it was then known. Yet doubters were confounded by later excavations which revealed that an older building, masked by conversions and additions, fitted the tale remarkably well.

The legend tells of a dishonest sacrist who fell into a moneylender's clutches. To repay his mounting debts he took the advice of a dark, cowled stranger who providentially appeared with a scheme for secreting and later re-selling partly used candles left burning by the faithful. There was one proviso: the first half-burnt candle taken from the shrine must be set aside for the stranger's use if ever he chose to call and collect it. If the sacrist himself were ever to use it, he would then belong to the stranger for ever and ever.

It seemed a simple business. The sacrist's profitable little swindle with the candles kept him going comfortably for years. But one evening, having to hurry to the cellar in the course of his duties and finding no other light ready to hand, he snatched up the fatal, dusty half-candle and lit it. In the cellar his attention was distracted by an appetizing chicken on a dish. He settled down to gobble it up as quickly as possible before being discovered, and by the time he had satisfied his hunger the candle was guttering low. As it went out, there came a clatter of hoofs from the refectory stairs. A robed, cowled figure swept in to claim the sacrist. He swept up the palpitating wretch, dashed out his brains against a step—where, it is said, the bloodstain remains to this day—singed his flesh with a sudden flame, and disappeared in a suphurous cloud.

In 1953 the priory reverted to its original function, when Augustinian friars once more settled in.

Congested Nethergate Street widens as it leaves the town, graced by fine frontages on both sides. The Elizabethan chimneys above

Nethergate Hotel, once Clare House, merit a respectful raising of the eyes.

The swoop of a railway bridge over the desolate cutting plunges into a short, winsome street which is Stoke-by-Clare. The snug, uneven, multi-hued houses are slightly marred by several unexpectedly drab slate roofs, as though at some point in history there had been a miscegenation of Suffolk hamlet and Welsh mining village. When I last went through, a notice on the wall of a public house declared itself firmly for the twentieth century: *Chicken, Steaks, Scampi*. The road takes a sharp right turn before a widening green and a cluster of trees guarding the approach to the church and the gateway of a private school, which was once a Benedictine priory and then the home of the Elwes family. The Tudor tower beside the drive was not, as it may appear, a gatehouse but a dovecot, one of its walls studded with a portcullis design in grey brick.

The pulpit in the church, c.1500, is so narrow that it could accommodate only a priest much given to fasting. This was just as well, for the manorial family were notoriously mean and probably treated the incumbent as frugally as they treated themselves: one inheritor was known to have fastened paper across windows rather than replace broken glass, and died (perhaps of the cold) in 1789 worth half a million pounds.

Beyond this corner the main road defects into Essex for a couple of miles. A by-road to Kedington is more rewarding. The church here contains some fascinating pews, including the canopied Barnardiston pew with separate sections for men and women. There are also monuments to the Barnardiston family, generations of whom dominated this district. They were in the main severe Puritans, and it is said that the name 'Roundhead' was first bestowed on one of them. He was Samuel Barnardiston, whose short-cropped hair provoked from Queen Henrietta Maria the comment, 'what a handsome roundhead is there'. The sobriquet stuck. Samuel later became a prosperous merchant and Deputy Governor of the East India Company. He was involved in the Rye House plot to assassinate Charles II, but escaped with his life: he was imprisoned for some years, and released on payment of £6,000.

The pulpit could not be more unlike that of Stoke-by-Clare. It is a resplendent three-decker, equipped with an hourglass and a pole on which to hang a wig.

And so, in this south-western corner, to Haverhill.

CHAPTER THREE

Central Suffolk

Arriving in Haverhill, most people's first impulse will be to leave it as quickly as possible. The town sign boasts of growth. The streets speak of decay : though few go back further than late Victorian days, when a clothing factory caused considerable expansion, and most belong to recent decades, they already reek with the dispiritedness of an industrial slum. Haverhill was designated one of the progressive 'overspill' areas for London. Industry was to be encouraged to move in. Industry proved unenthusiastic. There are still no adequate access roads, and the surfaces of most of the existing roads provide an obstacle course to anything other than a tracked vehicle : indeed, one gets the impression that a large number of such must have passed this way, creating cavernous ruts, miniature quagmires and booby-traps for travellers with ordinary cars and ordinary tyres.

The understandable eagerness of residents to call it a day and leave could not be more clearly demonstrated than in the 'For Sale' notices which flourish like an indigenous shrub all over the town.

The main escape roads lead either into Cambridgeshire or up past the airfield at Stradishall to Bury St Edmunds. To follow the county border closely is difficult, involving a secretive tangle of minor roads linking diminutive villages. Each of these introverted little communities can both attract and repel. For the ordinary visitor an hour in any of them would be too long; yet too short. You must either slow on the way through, nod graciously at the surface charm and then drive on, or you must live here a lifetime.

Several of the more attractive village clusters are linked by the River Kennett. North of Lidgate the bank of the stream is crowned by a fine decrepitude of cottages, many stained with the damp rising inexorably from watercourse and earth, and with the results of flooding. Here and there are lurid contrasts between pink and white frontages and vertiginous roofing in blue corrugated iron. In Dalham the cottages are reached by pert little green-smeared wooden bridges echoing the hump of the old 'thank-you-main' stone and brick bridges, so called because a man who crossed was supposed to thank the bridge for its courtesy in providing a passage. Here the stream shapes the village and pulls the road close to its own contour.

Wellington lived for some years at Dalham Hall. Cecil Rhodes bought it for his retirement but did not survive to take up residence. His brother brought his horse here and built a village hall in memory of Rhodes.

At Moulton an old packhorse bridge rears above the Kennett, incapable of carrying modern traffic and leaving such tasks to an adjoining by-road whose fording of the stream requires careful negotiation. Often dry in summer, the watercourse can flood with alarming speed in winter. In the floods of 1968 it overflowed into its string of villages. The memory of the mud and mess was still vivid in the villagers' minds when the heavy snows of January 1969 began to melt and there was a threat of further inundation. Young members of the Conservation Corps moved in, camped in the snow and slush, and worked unceasingly to clear the channel, slashing vegetation and moving rubble. In the process they revealed that the local inhabitants could have saved themselves much distress if they had not so blithely piled old prams, bedsteads and rubbish into the stream.

Now the minarets and clock towers of stables and stud farms dot the fields like the chapels of some esoteric local sect—which, in effect, they are. Every road carries warnings about 'Racehorses Crossing'. There are also signs announcing that one is in Cambridgeshire, to be swiftly cancelled out by signs restoring one to West Suffolk. Here in essence is an island linked to its mother county by no more than a narrow spit of land, in apparent danger from any encircling attack by raiders from the Fens.

The courageous Iceni who, under Boadicea, defied and came close to defeating the Romans, had a settlement at Exning. When this was struck by plague during the first century they moved the community and its market to what in due course came to be known as Newmarket. The ridge and ditch of the Devil's Dyke were probably constructed in the seventh century during the Mercian attacks on East Anglia, to command the crucial western approaches; but it is tempting to visualize an older earthwork, the handiwork of the Iceni, along whose broad rampart they might have run their horses and chariots. Their coins bore the effigy of a horse, and to this day it is impossible to think of Newmarket without thinking automatically of horses, and almost impossible to spend any time fruitfully in the town if one is not interested in the subject. Lloyd's Bank does seem to have an unfair advantage over its competitors with its trade mark of a leaping horse, most conspicuously displayed on the glass entrance doors.

The clock tower commemorating Queen Victoria's Golden Jubilee stands on a traffic island at the Suffolk end of High Street, which slopes gently down the gutter-delineated lay-bys for hansom cabs, now occupied by parked cars, and climbs steeply towards another memorial, this one a fountain to Sir Daniel Cooper. Royal Appointment signs are resplendent above the street, leaving no doubt that this is Royal Newmarket. The finest set is over a butcher's shop which itself has a splendid façade of gleaming tiles and proud lettering. Shops of this calibre are as worthy of preservation and admiration as any more ancient relic. To a modern eye the only blots on the glistening features are those great full points which modern typographers have discarded from display lettering; but one would need to be very austere not to revel in the sheer bright confidence of it all. The 'Rutland Arms' also has its regal blessing above warm Georgian brickwork, with an attractive inner courtyard from which the echoes of stage coaches seem not to have died entirely away.

Racing may be said to have had its symbolic beginning here when the Prince of Wales who later became Richard II rode on the Heath against the Earl of Arundel. James I paid the district a visit in 1605 and, at once alive to its possibilities, encouraged the development of a racecourse. He speedily became so fond of it that London and affairs of State took second place. In this, Charles I proved a worthy successor. He added to the small palace which James had built in what is now Palace Street, instituted the Autumn and Spring meetings, and in 1634 initiated a Gold Cup race. Here Rubens and Van Dyck had to come to receive their knighthoods. When Parliament wished to deliver the declaration which led to the Civil War, it was to Newmarket that they had to send.

In Cromwell's time there was no racing, but the Restoration of the Stuarts meant also the return of horses.

Although it stands at the lowest point in the street, at the foot of the westward slope, there is no doubt that the most important building in the town is the red-brick Jockey Club, built in 1772 and enlarged, restored and remodelled over the years. The Jockey Club was founded to formulate rules of conduct on and off the course. In 1827 it established by legal action its right to warn persons off Newmarket Heath, and gradually extended its authority to cover racing throughout the country. In 1947 an Equine Research Station was established, and in 1961 a forensic laboratory was added to deal with cases of suspected doping of horses.

The National Stud, first situated in Ireland and then transferred during the Second World War to Dorset, was finally brought to its obvious home adjoining the racecourse (actually just in Cambridgeshire) in 1967. Its different units, well spaced to lessen the spread of any possible contamination, stand behind what is known as Rowley's Mile, after Charles II, who was dubbed 'Old Rowley' by women who likened his amorous exploits to those of a stallion of that name. The Stud is open to the public from April to September on Sunday and Bank Holiday afternoons, and between 11 a.m. and 1 p.m. on race days.

Although no great gambler himself, Charles fondly allowed his numerous mistresses to gamble and run up debts which only he could pay. The most celebrated of his ladies, Nell Gwynne, is supposed to have stayed in the white house with black shutters which bears her name in Palace Street. It is also said that there was a subterranean passage from this house to the palace which then stood on the other side of the road. If Suffolk were really as honeycombed by passages for lovers, smugglers and rebels of various denominations as it is reputed to be, it would surely have crumbled and sunk far below sea level by now.

Appropriately enough, Newmarket railway station was the last in the country to employ a shunting horse, who worked there until 1967.

The main road back into the heart of Suffolk goes through Kentford, on whose outskirts, at a crossroads, is still to be found the grave of a shepherd boy who hanged himself when accused of sheep stealing. It is not known whether he did this in despair over a false accusation or whether he was more terrified of public hanging or transportation than of suicide. To this day there are still people who tidy the grave and put flowers—often plastic flowers—on it. It is usually covered with good-luck offerings on race meeting days.

Lesser, wandering roads lead into a world replete with tantalizing names: Frog Hall, Wolfe Hall, Frizzelers Green, Birdsend, Wilsummer Wood, Honeyhill Farm ... Will those spidery yellow lines on the map lead to revelations or disappointments? 'Can't imagine living *there*', shivers the visitor, rashly accelerating along a manure-splashed lane. Or, 'Must be deadly here in the winter.' If you do visit, you need to establish the right tempo. It is essential to stay off those roads where time and the traffic behind keep pressing one along.

South-west of Bury, beside the road that carries unfortunates back to Haverhill, is Ickworth Park, for more than five centuries the home of the Herveys. In 1784, de la Rochefoucald wrote of the fourth Earl of Bristol:

He is a man of immense wealth and has intelligence, a lively personality and an excellent capacity for intrigue. But they say he lacks a sureness of purpose and the power of planning a scheme properly in his head.... All the Herveys, they say, are a little mad, and Voltaire, when he was in England declared that he saw three kinds of people—men, women and Herveys; which shows there is traditionally something odd about the family.

At this time the Earl was touring Europe, spending and tipping lavishly, in gratitude for which a large number of Continental towns and cities raised a Hotel Bristol. The judgment on his eccentricities is a sound one, though it was unfair to accuse him of lacking sureness of purpose. The Earl was also Bishop of Derry, and when in Ireland he was certainly purposeful enough in his obsessive building of rotundas. At Ickworth he decided to crown his achievement by commissioning a really sumptuous rotunda to house his collection of paintings, silver and furniture. Work began in 1794 and was still going on when he died in 1803. After some delays it was completed by his son in 1830. The domed, elliptical rotunda is connected by two curving arms to massive wings, with an overall stretch of about 600 feet. Within are splendid displays of family portraits, silver and furniture—just as the fourth Earl had dreamed it would be. The formal gardens are perhaps even more delightful. Under National Trust administration, house and park are open to the public on Wednesday, Thursday, Saturday, Sunday and Bank Holiday afternoons from Easter Saturday until the first week in October.

Another mesh of wayward roads links such minor pleasures as Hartest, Boxted and the Bradfields. Herbert Tompkins' *Companion into Suffolk* makes quite an understatement when it declares: 'The county ... embraces few straight roads of any considerable length.'

Hartest is most happily approached from the east, down the hill into the sheltering valley where the village green draws out the pastel shades of its flanking houses. Brick and weatherboarding add firmer notes. The chestnuts give the final perfect touch to the orchestration.

The moated hall at Boxted has been the home of the Poley family for more than 500 years, and the features of many of them are preserved in the church monuments. Sir John Poley fought the Spaniards in Elizabethan times and then spent 20 years in the service of the flamboyant Christian IV of Denmark. Outside Shimpling, nearby, there is an agricultural college in Chadacre Park. Lawshall really has a hall, with walls six feet thick, now converted into a farmhouse. There are tales (but of course) of a subterranean passage to Coldham Hall, which boasts, for once with truth, that Queen Elizabeth slept here.

The Bradfield hamlets sit in agreeable clumps of woodland. Bradfield St Clare is named after the helpmeet of St Francis of Assisi, and the church is the only one in England thus commemorating her. The moated farmhouse was once St Clare Hall. The unusual name of Bradfield Combust derives from the burning of the local hall during riots against the Abbot of St Edmundsbury in the fourteenth century.

To the south lies Cockfield, made up of a sprinkling of greens—Colchester Green, Cross Green, Oldhall Green, Button's Green and others—where Robert Louis Stevenson worked on his earliest essays while staying at the rectory and where he met Sidney Colvin, who was to give him so much encouragement and, even more important, practical help.

Almshouse Green leads us on to Thorpe Morieux, notable for a fine Tudor farmhouse and for its church with a thirteenth-century font, fourteenth-century wooden porch, and fifteenth-century tower.

The watchful driver may find his hands trembling slightly on the wheel as he enters Bildeston and is confronted by a signboard which reads:

Death & Sons
Building Contractors, Funeral Directors,
Heating Engineers.

I find the juxtaposition of funeral director and heating engineer particularly alarming in this context.

Bildeston has a steep, tottering High Street which takes a welcome breath at the opening into Market Place before resuming its climb. The jaunty clocktower with its tiny belfry and spire was authorized in February 1864 and finished in June of that year, which speaks well for the contractors and craftsmen of the time. Today the bell chimes the hours with a note like that of a cracked Anvil Chorus.

The 'Crown' hotel lurches unsteadily up one slope of a cobbled hummock and down the other, protected from the road by trim white railings. Another inn shelters, for two hours on one day a week, the branch of a bank. The irregularity of the street is made even more picturesquely uneven by the strainings and saggings of timbered weavers' houses, also much in evidence in Duke Street and Chapel Street.

The church of St Mary Magdalen is set some way from the village on a steep hillock. Its lofty position, together with its clear windows, ensure a bright interior even on a grey day. There are fine carved lions, birds and tracery. A memorial tablet preserves the name of Captain Edward Rotheram, a Northumbrian who commanded Collingwood's *Royal Sovereign* at Trafalgar in its plunge at the French line and its crippling attack on the huge *Santa Ana*. He died of apoplexy while staying with the local Wilson family at Bildeston House.

North is Hitcham, remembered for its most distinguished rector, Henslow, who in the early nineteenth century, a man before his time, founded schools in the area and encouraged the study of botany. He set up clubs and allotments, lectured, and worked on the establishment of museums both at Ipswich and at Kew. While professor of minerals and then of botany at Cambridge he inspired Charles Darwin and was instrumental in securing Darwin's appointment to the *Beagle*. Like many a devout clergyman, he was later appalled by Darwin's theories, but remained affectionate towards his remarkable pupil until the end.

On a loop off the A.45 lies Woolpit, whose name does not, as might be supposed, testify to an old connection with the wool trade. It is a corruption of the old Saxon description of a pit in which captured wolves were destroyed. Spruce medieval and Tudor buildings surround a tidy little green. On one side the 'Swan' hotel shows a yard entrance clearly designed for stage coaches. Woolpit white brick was famous and fashionable until well into this century, but weathered badly. After the Second World War the brickworks fell into disuse.

The tower and spire of the church, visible from some considerable distance, are strikingly different from the regional pattern. They date only from 1853, though standing on a Norman foundation. The great south porch leads into an interior resplendent with angels, painted saints and heraldic animals, especially angelic below the double hammerbeam roof of the nave.

The road loop referred to above is there now and will be there for future generations. This shunting on to a siding is, however, fairly recent: like Stratford St Mary, the village was a staging point on the

main highway until that was diverted along a wider by-pass. Now reunited with the village proper is Lady's Well, on the road heading towards Elmswell across the A.45. Here are a moat and spring associated with Our Lady, their waters being held to work wonders on diseases of the eye. The revenues from pilgrims to this shrine were so valuable that Abbot Samson made a trip to Rome solely to ensure that they would be declared a monopoly of his abbey. There are pleasant footpaths across Woolpit Heath and on to Rattlesden past Clopton Hall.

Haughley is divided from its manor house of Haughley Park by the A.45 on its determined way to Stowmarket. A shadowy, flickering avenue of trees shields the road as it passes the park gates. The Elizabethan manor house, open on Tuesday afternoons between May and September, was ravaged by fire in 1961 but has now been rebuilt. The park also accommodates an egg-packing station.

Unless tempted irresistibly by the village names on one side or the other, we are now being channelled into Stowmarket, which could claim to be the true centre of the county. This busy little market town has no obvious architectural distinction but does breathe an immediately stimulating, bustling atmosphere. The Gipping was once navigable between here and Ipswich, and although its trade has now ceased the town has clung to its prosperity. Light industry encircles it but has not yet choked it. At the time of writing there is, and has been for some time, an impressive Danish design centre which might seem more at home in a larger city but which does excellent business in spreading Danish ideas and selling Danish furniture and fabrics.

At the west end of the church nave is a portrait of Dr Thomas Young, Milton's tutor who, on becoming vicar of Stowmarket, frequently had the young Milton to stay with him.

The grounds of Abbot's Hall, a short distance from the market-place, have been developed in the last few years as a museum of rural life in which are collected objects relating to the country scene past and present. Records are kept of customs and traditions which might otherwise be ploughed under, and a representative selection of farm implements, buildings and machinery of all periods is being built up.

15 Dennington: the Bardolph chapel (1440-1450)

In time the area may take on the appearance of those colourful, authentic and wonderfully un-dead open-air museums so lovingly constructed and tended in Scandinavia. My young son's earliest memory of Stowmarket is of a special week when traction engines were brought out on exhibition at Abbot's Hall: while his mother and I vainly tried at intervals to coax him towards the fascinations of corn-dolly making and the displays of old domestic and agricultural tools, he raptly studied the gentle to-and-fro of pistons and revelled in the mellow mechanical throb and the gorgeous smells of oil, steam and warm metal.

On the rising ground above the town, Stowupland offers one of the gems of the district—the moated farmhouse, Columbine Hall, flint and plaster with an oversailing upper storey.

Suffolk has well over 500 moated buildings of one kind and another, most of them farmhouses nowadays. In certain obvious cases the moat was dug for defensive purposes, but in many others it was designed for drainage or resulted naturally from the excavation of clay needed for the construction of house and outbuildings.

South of Stowmarket is Battisford, surrounded by its various 'Tyes'—another word for the Greens we have already encountered elsewhere. Sir Thomas Gresham, born in Norfolk, acquired the manor here and took from the estate the timber he needed for building his Royal Exchange in London. His predecessors had already made their mark on the City: his father, gentleman usher and money-lender to King Henry VIII, was Lord Mayor, and his uncle was Sheriff; but Thomas outshone them. He traded with the Continent, negotiated loans for the Crown, acted as a spy, and as a side-line indulged in some complicated currency smuggling for the benefit both of his country and of himself. At his own expense he undertook the construction of the Exchange on whose plans his father had worked up to the time of his death; and, according to the account in John Stow's *Survey of London*,

hee on the seventh of June 1567 laying the first stone of the foundation, being Bricke, accompanied with some Aldermen, euery of them laid a piece of Golde, which the workemen took up, and forthwith followed vpon the same with such diligence, that by the moneth of November ... the same was covered with slate, and shortly after fully finished.

Near at hand is Barking, whose proud medieval church with its gargoyles and internal woodwork, including a unique rood screen, recalls days when it was of some consequence, before river and road gave precedence to Needham Market. The habit hereabouts of pre-fixing the name of an inn with its place name—'The Blyford Queen' rather than 'The Queen's Head, Blyford', or 'The Shadingfield Fox' rather than 'The Fox, Shadingfield', for example—produces some oddities here. It is reasonable enough to talk of 'The Barking Fox', but 'The Barking Blackbirds' conjures up a strange picture and a stranger sound.

Needham Market is a double file of houses down the main New-market-Stowmarket-Ipswich road, with only the briefest vestiges of side streets. The first bank in East Anglia was opened here in 1744 by a Quaker merchant named Samuel Alexander. He soon moved on to Ipswich, which became his head office. The flint-walled church, squashed like everything else hard against the main high-way, has a tiny mockery of a clock tower and little else to distinguish its exterior. For that matter, it has little to commend its interior apart from the famous hammerbeam roof. This has been described as 'the culminating achievement of the English carpenter', but seems grandiosely out of place above this bare chapel, and was not always so highly regarded: at one time a plaster ceiling was installed to hide the 'barbaric' roof, and when it was removed in Victorian times the whole structure had to be dismantled and rebuilt with a great deal of new timber. The fabric has an air of making a great effort to hold the woodwork in place rather than the wood playing a support-ing role.

To the east of the A.45 the countryside remains mellow. The road to Coddenham performs an alarming flurry of turns under the rail-way and over the river, and then skirts Shrubland Park, rich with chestnuts and with terraced gardens below the Italianate hall conceived by that same Sir Charles Barry who designed the Houses of Parliament.

Coddenham, the Roman *Combretonium*, lies with understandable complacency in the lee of gentle hills. It is charming, and knows it. I have been through it at night and marvelled at the beauty, caught briefly in the headlights, of that splendid lower corner where an old inn has been turned into two fine bright houses, and the steep climb of the pargeted and timbered houses with their steps and railings. And I have been through it in daylight, in rain and in sunshine, and have never failed to feel a jolt of pleasure at the mere sight of the place. The larger old inns have ceased to be, but there remains the affable 'Duke's Head', a true 'local' with, on the wall of the public bar, an apposite sketch donated by the cartoonist Giles. The present landlady came here 65 years ago when she was a child of four, and has seen no real point in seeking any other home. Her husband, she admits, is still a bit of a foreigner: he comes from Needham Market, all of three miles away. Things, she regrets, are not what they were. In the old days people spent more time in the pub and talked a lot more instead of watching television. When it rained on a Monday (why a Monday? ... we didn't think to ask) the men on the roads used to come in and spend the whole day in the pub out of the wet, drinking and eating cheese and onions and 'talking about everything under the sun'. I did not, personally, get the impression under these rafters that the art of cheerful conversation had really died out or even that it was seriously ailing.

A Roman road from Baylham ran through Coddenham on to Peasenhall. Its line follows the valley north of the village, and the modern road to Pettaugh sticks pretty closely to it. The two then diverge but come together again near Earl Soham, proceed to Saxtead, part, and once more join up at Badingham, from where there is a lumpy but straight run to Peasenhall. The road coming in from Pulham St Mary is built on another Roman track. The two link up and head for Yoxford, where traces of the originals fade out.

There are several exits from Coddenham, all of them narrow. One lane is prone to flooding. These minor hazards have never deterred me from coming back, always with a sense of anticipation.

16 Heveningham Hall: Wyatt's neo-classical entrance hall (1781-1784)

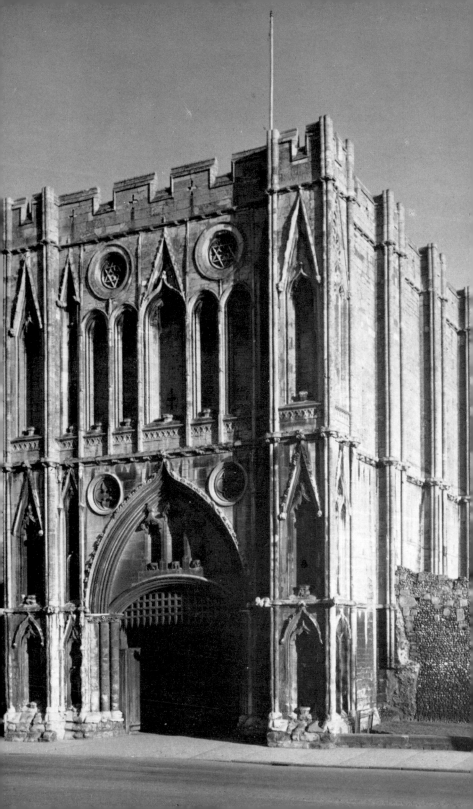

Along the verges of the approaches to Helmingham, or set well back behind orderly gardens, appear a number of bright little dolls' houses all based on the same pattern. They look like semi-detached almshouses, not lined up in staid, functional terraces but dainty and intelligently spaced out. These were designed as model cottages for the estate of Helmingham Hall, whose imposing Tudor gatehouse rears up suddenly above a shallow declivity. Framed within the red-brick gateway, a drive descends the slope and climbs again to the red façade of the hall, driving in through an entrance below a white-rimmed oriel window. The hall, which has quite a French swagger in this Suffolk countryside, retains its moat and drawbridge, and the park is still well stocked enough to warrant the nearby traffic signs warning against wandering deer.

The original house—one cannot but think of the existing culminatory building as a château—became the property of the Tollemache family in the late fifteenth century, and with few gaps the family has been in occupation ever since. In recent times a Tollemache invested in a brewery, which eventually combined with a rival to produce the name of Tolly Cobbold, hardly to be missed by even the most unobservant or the most sternly teetotal visitor to this part of the world.

The jaunty cottages continue in groups towards Framsden, overlooked by a post mill which for some years looked forlorn with its two remaining sails. Then repairs were carried out by enthusiastic young people, assisted by visitors' donations. On Easter Monday, 30 March 1970, the sails turned again, reaching at one juncture a speed of 30 miles an hour.

Now the signposts on all sides begin to nudge the traveller towards Framlingham. It is a welcoming town with an attractively tilted market place, a jumble of pantiled roofs, good antique shops, a good bookshop, and the agreeable 'Crown' hotel, a sixteenth-century inn partially reconstructed two centuries later and altered not long ago with care and good taste. The church contains the tombs of the Howards, dukes of Norfolk and their ladies, and that Howard who was the poetic Earl of Surrey, beheaded in 1547. The public

17 Bury St Edmunds: fourteenth-century Abbey Gate

school, Framlingham College, was founded in memory of Albert, Prince Consort.

All other features are dominated by the castle. There are grounds for believing that fortifications existed here in the times of Edmund, in all probability overrun by the Danes. The first definite records, however, are those of 1100, when King Henry I gave Framlingham to Roger Bigod.

The name of the Bigods is reputed to have originated with Rolf the Ganger, a Norseman who devastated the French coasts in the tenth century. Implored by his people to reach some sort of truce, Charles the Simple offered his daughter in marriage to the invader provided he would become a Christian. When agreement was reached, Rolf was commanded to genuflect and kiss the King's foot. He refused to bow to any man, but grabbed the royal foot and jerked it up towards his mouth, growling: 'Ne se bigod.'

A hundred estates were already in Bigod hands, gratefully awarded by William the Conqueror. Granted Framlingham, Roger built a wooden dwelling protected by a ditch and palisade. His second son Hugh supported Stephen, but soon grew arrogant and rebelled against his patron. He was pardoned and created first Earl of Norfolk, but again played the traitor and transferred his allegiance to Henry II. His appetite for disloyalty not yet sated, he clashed with Henry in 1157 and again in 1173, when he opened his gates to the Earl of Leicester and his Flemish army in their campaign on behalf of the King's troublesome sons. Leicester was defeated, and Hugh sought forgiveness. Henry decreed that his castles here and at Bungay should be dismantled.

Another Roger, son of Hugh, rebuilt Framlingham in solid masonry, and his are the existing walls and towers. Indulgence in the family habit of quarrelling with royalty, this time King John, resulted in his fortress being besieged and once again captured in 1215.

So it went on in its pattern of feud, rebellion, reconciliation, and renewed outbursts. When the last quarrelsome Bigod died, all his estates passed to the Crown. Framlingham changed hands many times over many generations. It came into the hands of the Howard family but was soon snatched away by Henry VII because they had supported Richard III. Thomas Howard, Earl of Surrey, after the spell in the Tower of London which appears to have been obligatory for all ambitious noblemen in those difficult times, had the castle restored to him, succeeded in defeating the Scots at Flodden in 1513 and was made Duke of Norfolk. The helmet he wore in the battle is preserved in the church. He spent his retirement in luxury at Framlingham.

The most celebrated occupant was Mary Tudor, who had been given the castle by her brother, Edward VI, and who took refuge here when he died in 1553 and it seemed that supporters of Lady Jane Grey might succeed in seizing the throne. Mary sent an order to the Council asserting her own royal claim. In reply, Northumberland marshalled troops and marched out of London to confront her. Mary unfurled her standard, a rising in the Midlands intercepted Northumberland, and with the support of many East Anglian knights Mary marched unopposed on London. Many a loyal servant was later to regret his devotion. During Mary's reign, 36 people died at the stake in Suffolk alone.

Bringing the scales down hard on the other side, Elizabeth used the castle as a prison for recusant priests. In the seventeenth century it was bequeathed to Pembroke Hall, Cambridge, when the hall was converted into a poorhouse and most of the other internal buildings were pulled down, leaving only the walls, gatehouse and towers. Some of the discarded material contributed to the rebuilding of Southwold after its annihilating fire of 1659.

Today the ruins are classified as an Ancient Monument. They consist basically of three enclosures—the castle itself, with a ditch and wall, set into an outer bailey ringed by another ditch, and the Lower Court, flanked on the west by an artificial lake. One of the most interesting features, for visitors who do not suffer from vertigo or from my own pessimistic belief that I have only to set foot on a structure which has lasted for centuries for it at once to collapse, is the wall walk. This is reached by a spiral stairway and provides an uneven but finely panoramic course around the top as far as the ninth tower. The open gorges below these walks were originally covered by the buildings of the bailey and enclosed above this by timber framework and boarding. The flourishes of brick chimney still remaining are purely ornamental.

Any direction taken from Framlingham will offer its rewards. Parham has its moated grange, now a farmhouse. Letheringham watermill, in a sylvan setting near Easton, is open to the public on Sunday, Wednesday and Bank Holiday afternoons through the summer. Earl Soham drowses in its diminutive valley, curled around its splendid church tower. Colours and textures seem richer here than in almost any other village in the county—assiduously repainted window-frames, pink and white washes, deep thatch and glowing tiles, set off by a profusion of trees. The green was once the setting of an annual stock fair. Its falconer carved in oak was erected by the Women's Institute to mark the coronation of Queen Elizabeth II.

Heading from Earl Soham towards Yoxford, we soon climb out of the lushness of this little community on to an exposed, often windswept plateau. There was a time when this wind was well employed : thrusting up from Saxtead Green is a beautifully preserved post mill, still in working order and now maintained by the Ministry of Public Buildings and Works. Visitors can climb a wide wooden ladder into the buck, or body. This is of white weatherboarding, set upon a brick roundhouse. The brickwork has been raised on more than one occasion to give safer clearance between the sail tips and the ground. The buck is controlled by a fantail at the rear which, driven by the wind, in its turn rotates a wheel along a circular track to keep the main sails facing into the wind.

Another village dominated by its towering church is Dennington. It was in a shabby state before and after the last war, and guidebook authors used words such as 'gaunt' and 'derelict' about it. Restoration since then has meant what it ought to mean : restoration rather than piecemeal refurbishing. The two fifteenth-century parcloses have a lacy delicacy. A pyx, with canopy and original cover, is operated by a simple pulley system before the altar. There is a riot of fine bench ends, one of which is adorned with the only known medieval carving in England of a sciapod, a fabulous creature ('found, if not in Africa, then somewhere else', says M. R. James mysteriously) with only one foot, on which it hopped when it wished to travel and which it held above itself as a sunshade when it wished to lie in the desert and rest. A sand table demonstrates an early method of teaching children to write and do their sums, with an erasing board to restore the smooth surface. On a great alabaster tomb lie effigies of the Lord Bardolph who fought at Agincourt, and his wife; his feet rest upon a hawk, hers on a wyvern.

Badingham 'White Horse' is an attractive inn set back from the road just as it makes a steep climb and steep turn before striking out once more against wide, unsheltered farmlands.

Peasenhall, like Polstead, is known beyond the county borders as the setting of a famous crime. Several studies of the case have been written, and even within the 1960s at least three novels have been constructed around the baffling events. Still nobody has provided a convincing solution to the murder of Rose Harsent in 1902, though it is not hard to find people in the village who will mutter, 'Well, what my dad always said ... what my grandma wanted to know was *why* ...'

The backbone of Peasenhall is a long street with houses and shops on one side and a stream-cum-drain on the other, with a straggle of houses beyond the water, picturesque or unkempt according to your taste. The side lanes have some pretty cottages and some drab ones. Langdale House is a sturdy Regency building; the 'White Swan' has good timbering inside, masked by the roughcast exterior. Although it has never grown to be more than a thin, strung-out village, Peasenhall had its days of comfort and reasonable prosperity: in 1800 the firm of James Smyth and Sons Ltd developed the Suffolk or Peasenhall drill, a corn seed drill which brought aid to farmers and profit to the village. The works, with one wall rammed hard against the churchyard, have been closed for years now.

It would not be true to speak of a depressed area, but perhaps we might fairly say that the place has sagged somewhat. Yet though it offers few special attractions to the student of architecture or the browsing sightseer, there is in its faded charm a sense not so much of a lost past as of a quiet, unflustered will towards self-preservation. The quietness is, it has to be admitted, rudely shattered at intervals when the current enthusiasm for stock car racing breaks out: for some reason Peasenhall has become an acknowledged centre of this sport.

Where 'the street' of Peasenhall ends, Sibton begins, rising to its village emblem by the church. This, one of the many well-conceived and well-wrought signs in this part of the county, recalls the existence of the Cistercian abbey which was founded in 1150 and has now crumbled into a few lumps of stone wall, doorways, windows and coffin slabs in the parkland below. It became the property of the second Duke of Norfolk (grandfather of Henry VIII's fifth wife, Catherine Howard), who generously granted pensions to the dispossessed abbot and his monks.

The slender, wispy river Yox runs towards that forgotten ford which long ago gave a name to the village of Yoxford, before flowing on to become the Minsmere. Known as 'the garden of Suffolk', though with little more right to such a title than many another beautiful parish, Yoxford is cushioned by luxuriant parklands, the last of their kind before the A.12, beyond which fields shade off into heathland and marsh, whispering and smelling of the sea. The wavering street along which this 'thoroughfare village' has grown up sports some precarious-looking wrought-iron balconies, bow windows, and the inevitable colour-washed walls.

On one of the inns appears the name of the Blois family, which has occupied Cockfield Hall since the seventeenth century. The original Tudor building has been remodelled and modernized many times, but retains its sixteenth-century north wing and gatehouse. A Victorian lodge stands by an entrance from the village itself. Here in 1568 died the last of Elizabeth I's rivals.

Elizabeth was the last to survive of Henry VIII's children, and if she died without heir the succession would have to be through descendants of one of Henry's sisters. Henry himself had pronounced in favour of his younger sister Mary, who married first Louis XII of France and then, on being widowed, the Duke of Suffolk. One of her descendants had already suffered tragically at the hands of Bloody Mary. In their attempt to keep Mary Tudor from the throne, Northumberland and his confederates had attempted to have Lady Jane Grey, the Duchess of Suffolk's eldest granddaughter, declared Queen.

In due course Lady Jane and her father, the Duke of Suffolk, were executed. The second granddaughter, Lady Catherine Grey, still had a strong claim if Elizabeth should die childless—or should be removed by plotters.

The Suffolk line was more favourably regarded by most Englishmen than that of the scheming Mary Stuart, Queen of Scots, daughter of Henry's sister Margaret. Conspiracy was in the air. When Catherine secretly married the Earl of Hertford, Elizabeth suspected that this must all be part of a plan to set up a contestant for the throne should she, the Queen, marry Dudley, as she was rumoured to be contemplating. She summarily declared Catherine's marriage void and sent both her and her husband to the Tower, where in due time they had a first and then a second son. Her health deteriorated, and Elizabeth finally relented so far as to send her to Cockfield to recuperate. She did not survive long, and was buried in Cockfield chapel, to be removed during the reign of James I and interred beside her husband in Salisbury Cathedral. So ended the royal hopes of the Suffolks.

The grounds of Cockfield force the A.12 round a tight curve, threatening to strangle Satis House. This, too, has had its feminine drama. It was bought in 1878 by a Mrs Clarissa Ricketts who, separated from her husband shortly after marriage, bred racehorses and loved to drive in a brougham through Yoxford with her dogs seated beside her. She also loved gambling, and in 1887 went to Monte Carlo to make a fortune out of a system in which she had great faith. Word reached friends at home that she was losing heavily, and shortly after her return she died, at the age of 47.

In accordance with her own instructions her coffin was carried to the churchyard in her own carriage, drawn by two of her own racehorses. The dogs were put down and, by discreet arrangement with the sexton, buried in her fresh grave after nightfall.

There was much subsequent gossip about the death. The surgeon who signed her death certificate refused to answer questions. The man who made the coffin—not the recognized undertaker—moved away from the district. A contemporary reported that the racehorses drawing the carriage were unused to such work and bolted, tipping the coffin out so that it broke open to reveal a load of coal in place of a corpse. An anonymous supporter of another rumour pinned a notice on the church board:

> *Mrs Ricketts is not dead*
> *But two fat pigs were buried instead.*

There were assertions that Mrs Ricketts had been seen alive in the village, that she had been seen leaving Darsham station disguised as a man, and later that she was alive and well in Egypt. The coffin-maker, tracked down in 1920 by an interested enquirer, hinted that he had reason to believe she had committed suicide.

Catherine Grey was carefully guarded and probably had little opportunity to wander freely in the verdant environs of the village. Whatever the truth behind her death, Mrs Ricketts obviously had little pleasure in Yoxford after her return from Monte Carlo. We who are alive and free both from gaolers and from gambling debts are so much more fortunate. We have a choice.

The A.12 runs in one direction towards Saxmundham, which has an enticing name and little else; in the other it heads for Lowestoft on the north-eastern tip. Down the lanes on its far side lie the lost ports which succumbed centuries ago to the encroaching sea, and those other obstinately enduring ports which have withstood Vikings, Normans, Dutch, Nazis and the North Sea, and are now putting up a stolid defence against jukeboxes, amusement arcades and transistor-radio culture. Or, facing inland again, we look out over broadening farmlands, the great spaces north of the Yoxford to Newmarket road, their villages dour and less picturesque, leading eventually towards the prehistoric memories and intimations of the north-west border.

CHAPTER FOUR

Towards Bury St Edmunds

Large farms undulate far off into the distance as though to overwhelm property boundaries and gather up the whole earth in one unbreaking tide, surging on and on into Norfolk and engulfing it. These vast tracts of soil, fervently worked for all they can be made to yield, may be sombre and depressing even when crops leaven the darkness; but on a bright winter's day—and there are many such in this land of low rainfall and protracted sunshine—they acquire a spacious beauty, the dazzling surface of snow speckled like a curlew's egg with brown blobs of loam. This is a landscape of concrete water towers, silos, monstrous barns and abandoned airfields—'turnip country' to some scoffers.

Turnips are indeed the embodiment of what Defoe called a 'whole country ... employed in dairies or in feeding of cattle'. Apart from spasmodic light industry introduced recently into places such as Halesworth, the only really significant change of emphasis in 300 years has been in the extension of cornland due to the demands of two major wars. The production of foodstuff for cattle is still a key occupation. There has also been a long tradition of turkey breeding, though nowadays they are no longer driven by the hundred on foot all the way to London for the Christmas trade, as was once the custom. Another, more recent, seasonal rush takes place when peas are swiftly picked and swiftly transported to frozen-food packers in Lowestoft and Yarmouth.

In the heart of this well-husbanded country, near the source of the river Blyth and once the terminal of the now extinct Mid-Suffolk Light Railway, stands Laxfield. It has a timber-framed, brick-

19 Bury St Edmunds: (above) twelfth-century ivory cross made for Abbot Samson; (below) detail of the Moses medallion

nogged Guildhall, first recorded in 1461 as a 'cherchehous', donated by the lord of the manor for the use of a religious and charitable guild. After 1543 it was administered by trustees for the benefit of local paupers, and until the beginning of this century it still housed poor people. The broad church, without pillars, has roof timbers like those of some huge inverted hull, its appearance slightly marred by metal struts which once held oil lamps and proved too difficult to remove. Laxfield is celebrated not so much for its buildings, however, as for its infamous iconoclast, a rabid destroyer who lived to the undeservedly ripe old age of 82. It is generally supposed that he was born here, but one or two historians anxious for Laxfield's good name have tried to establish that he came here at an early age from Stratford St Mary, which so far has made no noticeable effort to substantiate this.

His name was William Dowsing. His influence on the ecclesiastical face of the county assuredly equalled and probably surpassed that of any single predecessor or successor. A Puritan zealot, he was appointed in 1643 Parliamentary Visitor to the Churches of Suffolk, with the task of destroying superstitious pictures, ornaments and all such trumperies. He lost no time. By April of that year he was some miles away in Bramfield, gleefully recording the items for destruction: '24 superstitious pictures: one crucifix and picture of Christ: and twelve angels on the roof: and divers Jesus' in capital letters: and the steps, those to the rood-loft, to be levelled.' Add the depredations of Dowsing to those of the Danes and, later, the earnest Victorian Philistines, and it is a wonder that so much of Suffolk's magnificence has survived.

Bramfield's round tower is set well apart from the thatched church itself. Its walls are three feet thick and, like many of the 160-odd similar erections in East Anglia, it was probably conceived as a defensive structure, with spiritual considerations coming a poor second. This is borne out by the provision in several such towers of entrances well above ground level. If a village were attacked, the inhabitants could drag themselves and their belongings up a ladder and then haul the ladder up behind them.

Within the church is an exquisite rood screen. The chancel con-

tains a monument most movingly portraying Elizabeth Coke with
a baby in her arms; the kneeling figure of her husband Arthur gives
a good idea of the armour of his day. Arthur Coke's father was the
lawyer and Lord Chief Justice, Sir Edward Coke, who owned the
manor of Huntingfield. Arthur himself lived in the original Brook
Hall, a mansion which has now disappeared but is believed to have
stood about a mile to the south of the present building.

Another body laid to rest here is that of Bridget Applethwaite,
once Bridget Nelson, whose epitaph is a novel in itself:

After the Fatigues of a Married Life,
Borne by Her with Incredible Patience,
For four Years and three Quarters, bating
    three Weeks;
And after the Enjoiment of the Glorious Freedom
Of an Early and Unblemisht Widowhood,
For four Years and Upwards
She Resolved to run the Risk of a Second
    Marriage-Bed
But DEATH forbad the Banns—
And having with an Apoplectick Dart
(The same Instrument, with which he had Formerly
    Dispatcht her Mother)
Toucht the most Vital part of her Brain;
She must have fallen Directly to the Ground,
(as one Thunder strook)
If she had not been Catch't and Supported
by her Intended Husband.
Of which Invisible Bruise,
After a Struggle for above sixty Hours,
With that Grand Enemy to Life
(But the certain and Mercifull Friend to
    Helpless Old Age.)
In terrible Convulsions, Plaintive Groans or
    Stupefying Sleep

79

Without recovery of Speech, or Senses,
She dyed on the 12th day of Sept. in ye year
(of Our Lord 1737
(of her own Age 44

The adjoining slab seems to indicate that there were some complexities in the sorting out of her financial affairs, and that her husband's treatment of her inheritance may well have contributed to the Fatigues which she bore with such Incredible Patience.

At the time of the Norman Conquest an oak stood here which features in several episodes of parochial history. It occurs in an old ballad singing of Hugh Bigod's flight after one of his tussles with the King, and was even then so celebrated that it needed to be referred to merely as the Bramfield Oak, without further gloss. In 1843, by which time it was estimated to be over 1,000 years old, its last two branches collapsed and brought it down, leaving only a stump.

Guarding one side of the present Brook Hall grounds is a typical serpentine or 'crinkle crankle' wall.

The roof of the church has many echoes in the vicinity. There are fewer thatchers than before the war, but the craft is by no means dying out. Mr Cyril Rackham of Bramfield was responsible for this work on the church, for a perfect roof by Wenhaston church, and for the outstanding local example, Thorington Round House, where a by-road from Bramfield joins the A.12. This latter won him the Kayler Cup in 1968 for what was adjudged the best thatch in Suffolk. 'I'm not saying it *was* the best', says Mr Rackham modestly : 'just that it was *adjudged* the best.'

Reeds are gathered between January and March from Southwold, Dunwich and Minsmere, cut and dried, then stacked ready for use. At the beginning of each job the roof is stripped down to bare battens, bundles of tied reeds are laid, fastened into place, released from their individual bindings, and then covered with another full layer of similarly secured bundles, and a third. Only at the ridge of the roof is it impossible to use more than one layer—'And that's where the birds get in'. The best way of keeping birds out is by laying a cover of wire netting, but this detracts from the design. Each

20 *Hengrave Hall (John Eastawe, c.1525): main entrance, with carving of Fishmongers' arms*

thatcher has his idiosyncrasies, especially noticeable in the straw topping of the whole construction. Mr Rackham favours a frieze of inverted triangles interspersed with half loops. 'What I like doing most of all is eyebrows.' It is an apt description of the small but often complicated arches over dormer windows.

Insurance companies are wary of thatch, yet there are proportionally no more fires in this than in any other kind of roof. And, as its admirers will tell you, reed has a lifetime of wear in it. Mr Rackham is called in to re-thatch a huge barn classified as an Ancient Monument; to restore a tiled or slated cottage to its former state; and goes as far afield as Northamptonshire and Sussex to help people who, having seen the real thing, want it for themselves.

Thatched roofs add distinction to many modest little village pubs. The Blyford 'Queen's Head' is neatly set back from a tricky road junction, facing the church on the far side of the main curve. Approached from Wenhaston, both inn and setting present a picture no painter would dare to invent. Blyford, close to the river Blyth, was once Blythford. The queen represented on the inn sign is meant to be the wife of King Anna, a Christian Saxon who was slain by a pagan Mercian at the battle of Bulcamp Heath, his corpse being ultimately carried away along the road still known as King's Lane.

This was a focal point of local smuggling. There were many ruses to conceal stocks of contraband from the Excisemen, and by this time it will surprise no reader to learn that there is a tradition of a secret passage linking inn and church. In this case, however, there may really have been some substance to the story. When alterations were carried out to the premises in 1969 and the old cellar was opened up, a blocked-up arch was found in the wall nearest the church. Nobody risked unblocking it.

More recently still, since the completion of these alterations, there have been tales of a haunting. Footsteps have been heard by the landlord, his wife, and regular customers in upper rooms when nobody could possibly have been up there. Suitable coaxing will often unleash hair-raising theories from these regulars.

On the subject of hair, raised or otherwise, it is worthy of note that on Thursday evenings this inn is also a haircutting saloon. A

21 *Redgrave: monument to Sir John Holt (d.1710)*

barber is in residence for the entire evening, providing local men with a foolproof excuse: any calculating husband can manoeuvre his wife into making rude remarks some Thursday about his needing a haircut, can just 'happen to think on' that the barber will be at the Blyford 'Queen' that very evening ... and can return after closing time shaking his clipped head and lamenting that there was such a queue he thought it would *never* get to be his turn.

Less than a mile away, Wenhaston merits a visit for its 'Doom', obscured for years under a coating of whitewash. It incorporates a vigorous portrayal of demons driving naked sinners into a hellish maw. The pious look rather bleached; the condemned women are considerably more fleshy. The presumably devout man who painted the allegory seems to have had something in common with those newspaper editors who denounce the permissive society while ensuring that accompanying illustrations are of the most sensuously provocative kind.

Another link in the smuggling chain is Westhall. The double roof of St Andrew's church encloses a gully which is conveniently invisible from the ground. On one occasion smugglers with the Revenue men hard on their heels used this to hide their casks. Thatchers working on the roof had left their ladders in position, and there was a plentiful supply of reeds laid out ready for continuation of the job, which came in useful to cover up the contraband. Given a small *pourboire* (in the exact sense of the word), the thatchers proved loyally quiet.

A post mill, at first glance cousin to that at Saxtead, rears above Holton on the way into Halesworth. The present nameplates proclaim the village as Holton St Peter, but this recent innovation has no historical justification. In spite of purists' protests, the local authority will not replace the signs at this stage: the ratepayers have already paid for the new version, and until the lettering wears thin they are happy to keep their pence in their pockets and their homes in Holton St Peter.

The mill, above its pink-washed, pargeted Mill House, is over 200 years old. During restoration by the East Suffolk County Council it was discovered that in its present condition the framework would

84

not support its authentic sails. To preserve the visual balance, and since no practical use of the mechanism was intended, special sails of a light box construction were devised and are now in place.

The church is another of those with a round tower, this one unusually slender.

Yoxford and Halesworth were perhaps once joined by a Roman road. Stone Street runs into Halesworth from Woodton via Bungay, culminating in what local drivers derisive of the speed limit refer to affectionately as 'the Bungay straight', and the general inclination of the road on the map would seem to indicate that it went on to join up with the Roman roads from Peasenhall into Yoxford; but there is no remaining evidence of it south of Halesworth.

Halesworth is a market town with a few pleasant if undistinguished corners. Even its pleasures are hard to study: the narrow streets twist so tightly and are usually so congested with delivery vans and lorries parked half in the road and half on the pavement that drivers and pedestrians alike have to concentrate on survival rather than sightseeing. The surroundings of the church are soothing, and the nondescript exterior of the 'Angel' hotel, set on a particularly hazardous bend, conceals a fine entrance hall and staircase, and several rooms of some merit.

The railway line from Ipswich to Lowestoft, passing through here, has several times been threatened with closure. According to a one-time general manager of the region, most of the deficit on this much-used line—the only one now going anywhere near the Suffolk coastal strip north of the Deben—is due to British Rail's legal obligation to staff and maintain a large number of small level crossings over insignificant side roads and lanes which weave to and fro and sometimes intersect the track a couple of times within a mile. The route has survived so far only by going over to the unstaffed halt, pay train system. Halesworth station, now such a halt, has had its ups and downs. When the platforms were lengthened in the busier days of 1922, sections on both sides had to be attached to movable gates across the road beside the station. Swinging these open for traffic, platform and all, was a far more cumbersome business than the operation of an ordinary crossing gate. Part of the building was destroyed by enemy action during the Second World War. Now the movable portions of the platforms no longer operate but are locked across the road, which has thus been chopped into two culs-de-sac. Since most of the infrequent trains nowadays are two-coach diesel units, this long stretch of platform looks somewhat incongruous.

Gone are the vigorous days of the old Great Eastern, which enjoyed almost exclusive rights in Suffolk after an amalgamation in 1862 of various smaller companies. The engines then had a sparkling blue livery and a flamboyant coat of arms incorporating the shields of Maldon, Ipswich, Norwich, Cambridge, Hertford, Northampton, Huntingdon and Middlesex. When the 'Claud Hamilton' class of engine was developed for the region, each carried a cast-iron plaque of the arms individually painted by girls from the Railway Orphanage.

The Ipswich-Lowestoft line may yet be condemned and go to join the Mid-Suffolk, which remained independent until the 1920s. Abolished in 1952, it has left a few jaunty little monuments—huts and cottages, unmistakable railway architecture, popping up unexpectedly in the middle of fields of grain.

Threats of extinction also hang over other, older local features. At the time of writing there stands in Quay Street, Halesworth, the home of Sir William Hooker, the famous botanist who was director of Kew Gardens and whose son Joseph, born here in 1817, was later to distinguish himself in the same field and to become Sir Joseph. The house may, however, not exist by the time these words appear in print. In view of its dangerous deterioration the owners wished some time ago to sell it, but East Suffolk County Council placed a preservation order on it. The Urban District Council then sought means of restoring the house to a reasonable condition so that it could be sold or let, but finally gave up. The County Council was persuaded to agree that the house should be demolished. In December 1969, the Ministry of Housing and Local Government announced that a public enquiry must be held before any further steps were taken. The U.D.C. protested violently on the grounds that this was 'a sheer waste of public money' and that further delay might endanger lives. Hooker House still stands—or, rather, sags—but nobody yet has decided what can possibly be done with it.

Problems of this kind have unhappily to be faced all over the country. It is not always, as emotional writers to the newspapers and architectural journals imply, a question of insensitive councillors or officials shrugging off their responsibility to maintain past glories: costs of preservation and upkeep are all too often prohibitive. The balance between expediency and the longing to preserve our heritage is a vertiginous one.

While this controversy bubbled in Halesworth, there was greater national concern about the fate of nearby Heveningham Hall, whose Corinthian north front looks down 'Capability' Brown's pastoral slope to the lake and the B.1117 beyond Walpole.

Sir Gerard Vanneck, son of a Dutch banker who settled in this country early in the eighteenth century, decided to convert the Queen Anne house on the estate into something grander. Sir Robert Taylor produced designs for the new hall, and the exterior was almost completed when young James Wyatt was commissioned to take over from Taylor. The ravishing green entrance hall, the library, much of the furniture, and the orangery in the grounds are the finest surviving examples of Wyatt's style, all the lovelier for being where they belong, in a harmonious whole. A fire in 1949 damaged the dining room, but restoration was carried out in accordance with the original designs, which had mercifully been preserved. Other of Wyatt's preliminary sketches and trial designs are displayed in an upper room.

In the 1920s the Hon. Andrew Vanneck acquired the estate from his brother, Lord Huntingfield, and on his death in 1965 left it in a discretionary settlement for his family. The new Finance Act, with its clause subjecting discretionary settlements to Capital Gains Tax, levied in increasing amounts on hypothetical appreciation of assets over the years, made private upkeep of the mansion impossible. In an effort to cope, the family opened the building to the public and staged such outdoor events as veteran car rallies; but even with an average of 30,000 visitors a year the losses were crippling, and it was decided to sell, with the possible break-up of the estate and the

fragmentation of Brown's seemingly informal but beautifully cal-
culated landscaping.

Three possibilities were mooted. A private buyer might retain
the house and estate intact; they might be taken over by the National
Trust; or the Hall and grounds might be adapted to the requirements
of an institution of some kind. But no private buyer came forward;
the owners could not afford simply to give away the property and
its contents to the National Trust and could offer no endowment for
its upkeep; there were not enough bedrooms for an institution, and
in any case the decoration which is one of the Hall's glories would
probably not survive the full-time use of the building in this way.

So Wyatt's masterpieces were to be shut away, the furniture sold
off, the orangery and stabling demolished, and moss and mildew to
be resisted no longer?

In April 1970 the Minister of Housing announced that Heveningham Hall would be bought for the nation. About 500 acres of land
would be included in the purchase, and Wyatt's furniture would also
be retained. The National Trust are caring for the property, and
plans for its future, which will obviously take some time to evolve,
are being discussed with East Suffolk County Council. The important thing it that Heveningham has been saved, and is open to visitors on certain days. The visitors include many inhabitants of the
surrounding countryside who would feel a keen sense of deprivation
if they could no longer make their regular, refreshing pilgrimage to
this treasure-house.

In every direction are hamlets which rarely attain the size of even
the most modest village. Agriculture is all. Huntingfield church
shelters the remains of the Vannecks and the Huntingfields, and
Queen Elizabeth is known to have stayed in the manor which once
existed here, wounding a deer which is supposed to have hidden
itself in the hollow oak tree still known as Queen's Oak. Ubbeston,
on the site of what may have been a Roman encampment, has a
church whose Norman nave carries a fine fifteenth-century roof.
Tiny Bedfield, Bedingfield and Monk Soham all have worthy churches
in attractive settings, the provision of whose congregation in these
sparsely populated expanses is a mystery.

Sixteenth-century Flemings Hall lies in a tangle of by-roads between Bedingfield and Kenton, with all the picturesque accoutrements the heart could desire—a moat, a porch fit for a college, half-timbering, and great chimneys leaning inwards from Dutch gables. It was once the home of the Bedingfeld family, staunch Roman Catholics through all troubles and persecutions, who are still to be found at Oxburgh Hall in Norfolk.

Another mystery is the survival of the local inns. There is no great surge of tourists along these roads, and local workers do not wander far from home. Some establishments nevertheless enjoy such custom that they have been known to stay open long beyond permitted hours, hoping that the local policeman may be occupied far away. During a recent prosecution of a public house known for its lax timekeeping, one witness for the defence did not help matters at all by testifying indignantly, 'Couldn't have been all that late when I got back, 'cos my missus she said, "*You'm* home early tonight".'

At Stradbroke, the name of the 'Hempsheaf'—a more reputable establishment than the transgressors referred to above—stems from a crop which, plentiful along both northern and southern borders of the county, was used during the later sixteenth century for the weaving of sacking and sailcloth in an attempt to counteract the wool trade's decline of prosperity.

Weaving of a different kind is carried on today in Debenham, where rush weavers can be seen through a window overlooking the rightly named Water Lane. The town is called after the river Deben, which gurgles with youthful exuberance beside and under its main street, in search of the gentle slope which will take it eventually to the wide sweep of Woodbridge and the swirling currents below Bawdsey. There is hardly an eyesore to be found on either bank of this river on its way to the sea; hardly, indeed, any spot which does not merit hours or days of contemplation.

Debenham's hill, with its flicker of colour washes and occasional timber, and the pollarded sentinels along one pavement, has echoes of Bildeston but the ascent is less steep and the road wider. Around the outskirts are several small manor houses and farmhouses boasting partial or complete moats: among them Kenton and Aspall, and most notably Crows Hall, best approached with due deference on foot.

Once away from this oasis, architectural pleasures are spread pretty thinly. Patches of twentieth-century villas supplement Victorian farmhouses, sagging barns, and fabrications of corrugated iron. The huge silos vie with electricity pylons. Mickfield's houses and trees appear in danger of being throttled by ivy. A blunt church tower, vast expanses of loam, the spindly finger of Mendlesham's television mast shivering against the sky—all are seen at their most impressive not in bright sunshine or a summer haze but on an April day when lowering clouds spit rain, darken with the threat of thunder, and then skittishly allow unexpected shafts of sunlight through. There can be a dozen different kinds of weather arguing overhead. Brightness emphasizes an encroaching dark; damp green glows against the heavy soil; the road begins suddenly to steam, adding its smell to those of muck-spreading, ditch weeds, smoke from burning rubbish. This Suffolk is still remote, in spite of its pylons and television aerials. It is not an area for those who like romantic mountain scenery, pretty painted villages, sumptuous downland or seascapes: here it is the spaciousness, the airy freedom, which must appeal—or appal.

The sea is far away, yet much of an immortal book about the sea was written in Wetheringsett, a little village of thatched cottages beside a tributary of the Dove. In 1589 Richard Hakluyt published his great work on the *Principall Navigations, Voiages and Discoveries of the English Nation*, which was not merely a patriotic exercise but a scientific study of the problems and perils facing sea captains on still uncharted oceans. He learned several foreign languages in order to talk to, and even more to listen to, sailors from all over the world. In reward he was offered various high positions in Westminster, Lincolnshire and even America. He chose instead to become rector of Wetheringsett, where he spent the last sixteen years of his life. For ten of these years he worked on the revision and enlargement of his book. Seafarers and adventurers came to this quiet little parish to recount their experiences. In 1600 the definitive new edition was ready. 'The ardent love of my Country,' said the author, 'devoured all Difficulties.' When he died he was not allowed to remain in Wetheringsett, but was taken for burial to Westminster Abbey.

At Gipping the place gave its name to the river, which later joins the Orwell, instead of deriving it from the river as in Debenham. The Tyrell family had lived here for some time before producing that Sir James Tyrell who is saddled with the blame for murdering the Princes in the Tower on the orders of Richard III. It is said that the chapel here was built by the murderer in expiation of his crime. As there is now a large body of opinion which holds that Richard III had nothing to do with the Princes' death in the first place, one wonders how much foundation there can be for these supposed sequels. What is certain is that Sir James himself came to an unhappy end: he was executed for helping Edmund de la Pole, Earl of Suffolk, to flee the country when his plots against Henry VII fell through.

The farmlands continue to Haughley and beyond, but Haughley itself merits a pause. Its village green is another of the sloping triangular greens we have already observed in so many other places. One can almost imagine some self-satisfied designer marching hither and thither in seven-league boots, stamping the pattern upon every hillock in his path. A more imposing mound behind the church and a few disparate chunks are all that remain of a great motte and bailey built by Hugh de Montfort, stormed by the troops of the rebellious Leicester and Bigod in 1173.

Beside the road leading north from Haughley through Haughley Green is Walnut Tree Manor, headquarters of the Soil Association. A few hundred yards further on is the entrance to Haughley Research Farms, based on New Bells Farm with its moated farmhouse from 1450 and its nobly spreading thousand-year-old oak, and two adjoining farms added by the Pye Trust in 1967–68. Painstakingly recorded comparisons have been made here over more than 20 years between food and livestock raised on artificially fertilized land, and food and livestock from a unique 75-acre section which has never been treated with synthetic fertilizers or sprays.

The Soil Association is the creation of people who believe that a comprehensive study of the whole soil-plant-animal-man relationship is needed before the unchecked spread of modern farming methods ruins our environment. Just how much contamination can we inflict on that environment without doing irreparable damage; and if there is a limit, how close are we to it?

Formed in 1945, the Association took over in 1948 the farms established before the Second World War by Lady Eve Balfour and the late Miss Alice Debenham. It is no collection of cranks. Organization of the experimental work is severely practical, unhurried, and unbiased. Even after these 20 years of intensive study no sweeping generalizations are made; but some significant results are beginning to show. The 'bloom' on cattle reared on the organic section is, even to the untrained eye, noticeably glossier than that on cattle from the synthetically treated areas. Cows produce more milk from a lower bulk of food on the organic section. Apples from the orchards—I will vouch for this—actually taste like apples.

Outside bodies such as university research units have been allowed certain facilities, including the removal of soil, fungi and food specimens. Contact is maintained with experimental groups all over the world. Some restrictions may soon, however, have to be applied. The organic section has been operated, as far as possible, under farming conditions where produce must be removed for sale, as a self-contained entity. An area farmed in this way provides a base for comparison with other systems, sometimes called a control. It obviously imposes grave limitations on farming management, for no commercial organic farmer deprives himself of manures brought in from outside to close the gap between what is taken out of the soil by crops and animals, and the requirements of next season's growth. Over two decades the section has been as nearly self-sufficient and self-maintaining as anything can be. Now the Association doubts whether, with its low yield of arable crops, it can be sustained for fundamental research purposes. Resources cannot be spent two ways at once. With some reluctance it has been decided to concentrate on the organic demonstration farm. If research material is wanted by other bodies in the country, other finance must be provided.

The passer-by may note with disfavour the contrast between graceful Walnut Tree Manor (where for some time lived that Captain Oates who gallantly walked out of Scott's tent into the blizzard) and the low, uninteresting, pale green single-storey building beside it. In fact this is a centrally-heated, air-conditioned, weatherproof paradise with an expertly prepared cuisine—exclusively for rodents. Known as 'the mouse house', it provides luxury accommodation for thousands of mice whose grandfathers and great-grandfathers have been fed on controlled diets from different sections of the farm complex. To ensure that results can never be falsified by temperature or light changes, or by outside power fluctuations, the unit has its own generator, and stringent precautions are taken to prevent anyone entering this Mickey's Manor with an alien germ, a fleck of chemical, the faintest suspicion of contaminated food, or a puff of contaminated air.

There are no snap judgments and no glib answers. The Soil Association works with gruelling patience. Every now and then comes a faint indication from the outside world that other people are beginning to take notice. In December 1969 the Minister of Agriculture ordered an urgent investigation to establish whether or not 'modern farming practices are damaging soil fertility and structure'. 1970 was internationally proclaimed Conservation Year. Better late than never. But how late *is* it? Soil, declared Lady Eve Balfour in the early days of this experiment, is the basis of civilization. No Suffolk farmer is likely to quarrel with this statement; but he and many others would do well to re-examine what they are inflicting on that precious, irreplaceable foundation.

Not far away, running up between Wetherden and Elmswell, is the boundary between East and West Suffolk. It slices Rickinghall neatly in two. I will not attempt to establish any significance in the relative placing of Rickinghall Inferior and Rickinghall Superior.

Beyond, roads converge on Walsham-le-Willows, which lives up to its name by sporting a fine fringe of willows along its branch of the Little Ouse. The churchyard has a rich, thick palisade of limes.

In May every corner is heavy with lilac, and the streets are dusted by a pink snow of blown blossom. The crossroads offer rewarding vistas in all four directions. The 'Six Bells' inn takes its name from the bells of the church tower. Church Street displays architectural styles from the fourteenth to the nineteenth century, including a weatherboarded Guildhall now split up into four cottages. The continuation of the street follows the diminutive river with the fidelity of Lidgate and its similar stream.

Inside the church, the nave roof has alternating tie and hammer beams. Medieval glass found wrapped in a newspaper dated 1805 has been fitted into the east window. There is a medallion to Mary Boyce, who died in 1685, one of the few surviving examples of the 'Crant' or 'Garland' which used to be hung above the seats of unmarried girls who had died, to be wreathed with flowers by the youth of the village on each anniversary of the death.

The busier traffic of the A.143 comes as something of a shock, growling and breathing fumes through Ixworth on its way to or from Bury.

Ixworth has the remains of an Augustinian priory founded late in the twelfth century and still retaining its vaulted undercroft and some later remains of prior's and canons' quarters. Certain East Anglian coach tours include a visit to it in their itinerary; individual inspections must be arranged in advance.

A more leisurely, rural road from Walsham is that through Badwell Ash (a fine hall), Hunston (mellow cottages), past Stowlangtoft Park to Pakenham, whose tower mill is one of the few still working for its living.

And so we arrive in Bury.

Even to write these words induces a glow of pleasure. 'The nicest town in the world', said William Cobbett, glad to stretch his legs after so much rural riding. 'I take Bury to be the most attractive town in Suffolk', said M. R. James. William Addison wrote: 'To alight in Bury is to feel you have arrived.' Before reading the opinions of any of these writers on the subject I had long ago discovered Bury St Edmunds for myself and expressed just such sentiments to a number of friends. I have been in and through Bury at all times of year, in all kinds of weather, and even the shattering of my car windscreen there on a bleak day of sleet and slush has not cast the slightest pall over my picture of it. When I approach it I find that I am saying to myself, 'Ah ... Bury!'

Defoe in his day was charmed by the town, slyly observing that the 'beauty and healthiness of its situation was no doubt the occasion which drew the clergy to settle here for they always chose the best places in the country to build in, either for richness of soil or for health and pleasure in the situation of their religious houses'. He goes on to more secular observations, noting that 'it is crowded with nobility and gentry and all sorts of the most agreeable company ... so there is the appearance of pleasure upon the very situation, and those that live at Bury are supposed to live there for the sake of it!' It was rumoured that many attractive ladies from Norfolk and Suffolk who attended balls and assemblies here were really offering themselves at market, eager to be bought if the bidding were high enough.

The town, set above the delightfully named watercourses of the Lark and the Linnet, preserves a pattern established in Norman times in conjunction with the abbey. References before those days are scanty. It was known as Beodericsworth or Beaduricsworth in the seventh century, when King Sigebert founded a church and monastery here, but attained little real importance until a wooden church was set up to house the body of the martyred Edmund, in honour of which the town was renamed St Edmundsbury. The saint's remains were moved in 1010 to escape the renewed attacks of the Danes under Sweyn, and then brought back in 1013 to be reinterred in a richer tomb, now untraceable. Reports of miracles at the shrine attracted pilgrims from all over the land and brought prosperity to the abbey and the townspeople.

In the following century Abbot Anselm wished to make a pilgrimage of his own, this one to the shrine of St James of Compostella in Spain. He never achieved this, but built instead a church to St James, precursor of the present church and therefore of the cathedral.

All over Europe monasticism reached the pinnacle of its power in these years. Few more influential men than Abbot Samson (1182–1213) have ever ruled a community: for they were indeed rulers, these divines, temporal as well as spiritual. According to the *Chronicles* of his chaplain, Jocelin de Brakelond, Samson owned the allegiance of 50 knights.

A year after his death, the town experienced what was perhaps its most significant, historic moment. On St Edmund's Day in 1214, in the presence of Archbishop Stephen Langton, 25 barons made their protest at the high altar against tyranny and misgovernment, and pledged themselves to unite in opposition to King John until he granted a charter of liberties which could never again be overridden or circumvented. Their detestation of the feeble yet dictatorial king was so intense that at one stage they even offered the throne of England to the Dauphin of France. At last Magna Carta was grudgingly accepted and signed, in June of the following year, at Runnymede. It was not quite the democratic document which later generations of idealists have liked to worship. It was devised to protect the rights of barons and knights rather than the peasants, craftsmen and townsfolk who worked for them and were all too frequently trodden down by them. Nevertheless its wording established concepts fundamental to the later evolution of English liberties.

Rebelliousness seems to have been in the local blood. The hallowed English sport of tax evasion flourished here. The women of Bury once belaboured monastic collectors with their distaffs, and in 1327 the whole populace revolted against the abbot's exorbitant tax demands and pulled down the abbey gate. They were soon compelled to rebuild it, and their handiwork is to be seen in the present splendid structure. During the Peasants' Revolt the abbey was again stormed. At one time and another many of its treasures were looted, including some famous illuminated manuscripts. Others that were spared fell under the displeasure of Edward VI, who ordered their destruction on the grounds that they were dangerously superstitious in nature.

At the Dissolution in 1539, the abbot was pensioned off and it is believed that the body of St Edmund was once more moved. Unfortunately there is no reliable record of this, and no trace of the remains has ever knowingly been found.

Records of the thirteenth and fourteenth centuries give a detailed description of one of the splendours of the abbey, an altar cross of walrus tusk about two feet high and fourteen inches wide, said to have been presented in memory of a murdered boy—perhaps that child Robert who was supposed, as in so many distasteful legends, to have been ritually killed by Jews. Somewhere about the time of Henry VIII's dissolution of the monasteries this crucifix disappeared. Henry had insisted on the preparation of itemized lists of monastic wealth, and if it had been on such a list its loss would hardly have gone unnoticed. In some mysterious way it had been removed before the inventory had been drawn up.

The likeliest explanation is that a French monk returning to his homeland had determined to take the precious cross beyond the reach of the greedy king. It is thought to have been hidden away in a French monastery until looted by the Nazis in 1940. After the defeat of Germany it turned up in Munich, in the possession of a Czech or Yugoslav who had survived the war there. He claimed to have bought it for a few hundred pounds from a British or American soldier who must, in his turn, have filched it from the Germans.

The cross was offered to the British Museum. There was no doubt of its authenticity. But the museum would not offer to purchase unless the seller provided more details of the man from whom he had obtained it. This he either could not or would not do. In the end the cross was bought for £250,000 by the Metropolitan Museum of Art, New York, and is now displayed in the medieval section, The Cloisters.

After the Dissolution, St James' and St Mary's were allowed to function as Prostestant parish churches. The abbey was sold into private hands, and for many years the owner allowed townsfolk, for a small payment, to bring barrows and remove the stones of the abbey for any purpose they chose. A good proportion of the older cellars in Bury are shored up with this material, and there are plenty of patches above ground; the entire wall of the car park behind the

Farmers' Club in Northgate Street, for example, consists of abbey stones.

All that is left of the once awe-inspiring foundation is a farrago of shattered walls, stricken arches and compacted rubble, crouching on the well-kept greens or clawing up in warped shapes reminiscent more of Easter Island idols or horror-story monsters from the mind of H. P. Lovecraft than the hallowed remains of a great Christian centre. Yet it is a joy to be here on a spring or summer day. If I think involuntarily, out of the blue, about Bury the thought is somehow always accompanied by the tang of lawns being mown on a hot day, clear and pungent after the intoxicating smell of roses and honeysuckle all across the county. When the buzz of the mower has subsided, the birds reassert themselves, and children laugh behind a bush or across the grass. The Appleby rose garden was presented by an American airman who fell in love with Bury and its environs while serving with the Eighth Air Force, who, he says, 'made possible the happiest summer of my life'. He wrote an unashamedly sentimental, discursive little book about those golden months, *Suffolk Summer*, and donated all the royalties to the upkeep of the garden.

The west front of the abbey presents some anachronisms. Learned societies, two Government departments and the borough council have been wrangling with increasing acrimony over the fate of houses built into the ragged remains of Anselm's original fabric. 'A series of meaningless encroachments', says a representative of the Ministry of Public Buildings and Works. To others the interplay of dead ruin with still habitable Tudor and Georgian buildings creates a piquant beauty in itself. Most would agree that the few Victorian additions have nothing to commend them. Even so, will the walls look better if these intruders are wrenched out? Should all these rare examples of infilling be preserved; or should they be unpicked so that what is left of the authentic abbey may be exposed to view?

If the later houses were extracted from the walls to which they cling, we should be left with a jagged formation as impressive as those stony fangs already isolated on the greensward—as impressive, and possibly as incoherent. A crone with only three yellow teeth tilted at varying angles may be 'authentic', but might she not look

22 *Wingfield Castle: fourteenth-century south front*

more pleasing with a reasonably matched set of false teeth, particularly if she has adjusted comfortably to them for something like half her lifetime?

'An incongruous muddle grievously masking the great triple western doorway', says one faction.

'The ruins without the houses would look awful', says Sir John Betjeman on behalf of the other, 'like a bomb site with mown laws and litter baskets round it.'

The borough council, faced with the fact that the premises have for long been let at uneconomic rents and that the cost of much-needed repairs could be a heavy burden on the ratepayers, is in favour of demolition.

An armistice has been declared. The infillings have been reprieved until at any rate the end of the 1970s.

In 1914 the church became the Cathedral of St James the Greater. By this time it had been substantially altered. Nave and chancel were rebuilt in the nineteenth century. The great Norman bell tower remains, but is self-consciously separate from the body of the church and ringed by unworthy railings. A sculpture of Christ was removed from the archway at the end of the eighteenth century to provide clearance for loads of hay. Even without the railings, traffic today would have difficulty in passing through: the tower stands in a declivity, the result of raising the surrounding ground after floods.

The Victorian chancel has now been demolished, and a new choir and side chapels built. The new stone comes from Somerset, but Suffolk flint has been incorporated for characteristic ornamentation. Bright armorial shields bear the emblems of the Magna Carta barons, the cost of their carving and painting having been met by an American Society, the Dames of Magna Carta. A central tower and transepts complete the re-creation (for it is little less) of the cathedral church. Work was finished in time for a Festival between April and November, 1970, the 1100th anniversary of Edmund's martyrdom.

Towns, parishes and schools from all over the county have for some years been supplying tapestry-covered hassocks, their individual treatments being disciplined by the basic blue of the design and the old Christian 'Y' symbol. Within this framework there is still

23 *Blundeston: painted screen*
24 *Barsham: Norman tower on Saxon base, with modern thatch*

plenty of scope for the use of local emblems and for variety in the stitch employed.

Just as there have been dissensions concerning the west front, so there are still grumblings in the town over the choice of St James's as the heart of the diocese. St Mary's has always had vociferous supporters. 'A much finer building', said M. R. James in 1930. 'One of the most beautiful churches in the county', says Addison. 'One of the finest in the kingdom', says a more recent writer. St Mary's, too, owed much to Anselm, but the greater part of it is now fifteenth century, including the fine north porch donated by John Notyngham, a grocer. The claims of so many local patriots that *their* church, and theirs alone, has the finest of all hammerbeam roofs, meet a considerable challenger in the nave here, proud with saints, angels and kings. The remains of Mary Tudor, Duchess of Suffolk, were brought here from the abbey after the Dissolution and re-interred in the north corner of the sanctuary.

In the regimental chapel of the Suffolk Regiment hang the colours of what was once known as The Old Twelfth of Foot or, more generally and flippantly, 'The Swedebashers'.

When both the Duke of Argyll and the Duke of Monmouth threatened James II, he hurriedly raised new regiments for his protection. Among them was a corps which was to develop into the Suffolk Regiment, though at first it had no special connection with the county, which relied for its own defence on a half-conscript, half-volunteer militia. Volunteers for the new force were raised by Henry Howard, seventh Duke of Norfolk, in June 1685, but James soon developed suspicions of his loyalty and relieved him of further responsibility. Aware of widespread doubts and dissatisfaction, James decided to appeal personally to the religious and personal loyalty of his troops, and for this purpose had them drawn up on parade. He asked that they should all sign a declaration of submission to his authority. The Catholic Major, George Trapps, ordered those unwilling to comply to lay down their arms. To the King's horror, almost the entire regiment grounded arms.

While the regiment was being exhorted, organized, reorganized, and generally thrown into a state as confused as that of the King's own mind, its old Colonel, the Duke of Norfolk, came out on the side of William of Orange. In this he had most of East Anglia behind him. Once William was established on the throne, he appointed Colonel Wharton to the command of the regiment and despatched it to Ireland to deal with James' attempts to reinstate himself with the aid of the Earl of Tyrconnel's army. It was an ironically appropriate confrontation: Henry Wharton was author of that satirical ballad, 'Lilliburlero', aimed derisively at the Roman Catholic Tyrconnel while James was still in power. The Irish forces were soon hemmed in, but the lengthy siege brought depression, disease, 'and debauchery and drunkenness' to the Protestant forces. Wharton himself died of fever, and the regiment was under the command of Richard Brewer when it took part in the attempted extermination of the Rapparees, Irish guerillas whose methods were to be echoed by many subsequent enemies of 'The Swedebashers'. In later centuries the regiment was, in fact, to make a speciality of anti-terrorist operations: it distinguished itself in Palestine and Cyprus, and for three gruelling years in Malaya.

More spectacular incidents in its history include the battles of Dettingen and Minden, the siege of Gibraltar between 1779 and 1782, and the battle of Seringapatam. One of its privileges has been the wearing of a rose on 1 August in commemoration of Minden.

In 1935 the chapel in St Mary's was redecorated for the 250th anniversary of the regiment's foundation. In 1959 an amalgamation with the Royal Norfolk Regiment produced the first East Anglian Regiment; and in 1963 the colours of the first and fourth Batallions were finally laid up in the chapel prior to the formation in 1964 of the Royal Anglian Regiment.

Not far from the remains of the old Gibraltar Barracks, on the opposite side of Risbygate, is a plague stone, close to the site of the gate which once stood here. At this and each of the other town gateways there stood in the Middle Ages a hospital—save for Westgate, an omission now rectified. The gates themselves were pulled down when agriculture began to flourish and access had to be provided for huge waggonloads of produce. During the Plague the stone on Risbygate was the focus of a grim market. People from the countryside brought food to the town but did not dare to enter the infected streets. The hollow of the stone was filled with vinegar, and into this the townsfolk dropped their payment so that the coins would be decontaminated before the farmers collected them.

Before that, the hollow probably formed the socket for a wooden cross, one of a series marking the boundaries of the abbey's freehold.

Still, everywhere, there are these reminders of the abbey's power, the long reach of its arm. The 'Suffolk Hotel' is an eighteenth-century rebuilding of an ancient inn belonging to the abbey. The celebrated 'Angel' itself, facing the abbey gate, now has a grill-room in vaults which must once have been part of the great foundation. Stories are told, need one add, of a mysterious bricked-up doorway and of a passage leading to other vaults below the abbey itself.

The main body of the present 'Angel' was built in 1779, but there are records of an inn on this same site as early as 1452, and later three such establishments stood here side by side. Mr Pickwick arrived here in fine fettle before continuing his travels towards Newmarket, and there is inevitably a Pickwick Bar—to which, even in this day and age, ladies are not admitted. On the spacious slope of Angel Hill was held from 1135 onwards the lavish Bury Fair, both fashionable and boisterous. It was abolished in 1871, and today the space is marked out by the geometrical segments of a limited-period car park, dominated by a deplorable signpost which looks as though it might once have stood beside a cinema organ in the period of Electric Palace Art Nouveau.

This grotesquerie is, apart from the cars, the only blot on the slope, whose proportions justify the name of Angel Place rather than Angel Hill. At one end is the Athenaeum, once the Assembly House, remodelled in its present form in 1804 with an attractive portico and an observatory cupola, and restored and refurbished several times over the years, including a great deal of internal work during 1969. Moving from this corner towards the 'Angel', we pass the house of Dr Hyde Wollaston, the chemist and physiologist, and a private house known nevertheless as 'St Edmunds Hotel', where Louis Philippe stayed in 1791.

25 *Burgh Castle (third century* A.D.*)*

At the road junction beyond the hotel is a modern chemist's shop with attractive windows and, inside, a royal coat of arms. The arms of Hanover are superimposed upon those of George III, and I have been told that they were presented to the establishment in gratitude for some wonderful potion supplied to a royal personage. The present proprietor will have none of this, assuring me that the premises have been a pharmacy only since 1840. His father did, however, supply a special influenza mixture to King Edward VII when he came to Culford to shoot, and this was always referred to as 'King Teddie's Mixture'.

Further up Abbeygate Street a photographic branch of the same firm still displays, in a niche at first floor level, an old trade sign of pestle and mortar.

Angel Corner is a beautiful Queen Anne house, now the property of the National Trust and the home of the John Gershom-Parkington collection of clocks and watches. These were bequeathed to the town by one of its natives, whose name must still strike an affectionate chord in the minds of wireless listeners from before the Second World War, in memory of his son John who was killed in that war.

Abbeygate Street has several notable shop fronts and windows, particularly those of two grocers whose richly stocked interiors give out that enticing smell which no supermarket can ever achieve. Many of the side streets are equally rewarding, even if only in intermittent stretches, such as those in Whiting Street and Guildhall Street. There are some Georgian frontages in Northgate Street; Eastgate Street and St Mary's Square are fascinating. Here as in other market towns the upper storeys repay study, having escaped the shop-front vulgarizations which all too often mask what was once worth seeing at ground level.

The best time to contemplate such beauties, unfortunately, is on early closing day or on a winter Sunday afternoon, when there is little traffic to block the streets, block the view, and clutter up Angel Hill and the graceful Chequer Square.

In the heart of the town are the Butter Market and Cornhill. Robert Adam's Town Hall, used as a theatre for many years until replaced by that Theatre Royal where *Charley's Aunt* received its first performance before an audience of five, would show up better if not hemmed in so tightly by its neighbours. The first impression of the Butter Market is one of overall untidiness. The usual chain stores jostle the peeling, scabby local shops in a jumble of ill-assorted styles. Figures of Agricola, St Edmund, Edward I and Edward VI look down from above the familiar lettering of Boots the Chemist. On market day, closed to traffic, the wobbly L-shaped place presents a colourful discord which is a welcome change from the metallic ranks of parked cars; still it is disappointing to find that the market, too, is shoddy and devoted mainly to the selling of reduced-price nylon shirts, denims and washing powders.

A disappointment? One needs a sense of proportion. Bury is a working town, not a carefully preserved showpiece. If it has faults, they are less blatant than those of most contemporary country towns. So far as I am concerned, it makes up for all its failings by its warmth and liveliness.

To one side of the market is Moyse's Hall. It was supposed at one time to have started life as a synagogue, but there is little to support this theory, and it is likelier that it may simply have belonged to a Jewish merchant who gave it his name. Even this can be contested: Mr A. R. Edwardson, the present curator, points out that Moyse and Mose were perfectly ordinary Suffolk names in earlier centuries.

The building is constructed of flint and rubble with a Barnack stone dressing similar to that used in the abbey church. It may have been used as a guest house by pilgrims visiting the abbey. Certainly in later life it was to fulfil many purposes: an inn, private house, wool hall, workhouse, and bridewell. In the nineteenth century a proposal was made in the local council that the ground floor should be cleared and converted into a fire brigade station. This suggestion was defeated by only one vote—a vote which preserved the building and led to its adaptation instead as the borough museum.

The whole history of the county is summed up here imaginatively and unstodgily. From prehistory there is a fine display of blades, picks and mace heads from the surrounding districts and further afield. In the specimens assembled here it is possible to follow the development of arrowheads, spearheads, crude and not-so-crude farm and domestic implements. There are Roman coins, spoons and brooches, and some remarkable finds from the Anglo-Saxon cemetery at West Stow—bronze cruciform brooches of delicate workmanship, amber and glass necklaces, and well-turned bowls and urns.

Domestic souvenirs from many centuries are more moving, in their way, than many imposing relics: Queen Anne slippers, wig curlers, nutmeg graters; an ivory-handled nineteenth-century umbrella; silk embroidery and a shawl belonging to Agnes Strickland, author of *The Lives of the Queens of England*; 'Cherry Tooth Paste, patronized by the Queen'—and bearing a picture of the young Queen Victoria. The Bury labels and billheads are fascinating examples of florid typography. Near the entrance are the relics of William Corder, the Polstead murderer who took more than eight minutes to die outside Bury gaol before an audience of thousands. After the hanging his body was exhibited on a trestle table in the Shire Hall.

In the Traverse, parallel to Cornhill, is Cupola House. Originally built as a private house in the seventeenth century, it is now an inn with a restaurant and an attractive little room within the cupola which gives it its name. The plaque to Daniel Defoe above the entrance would seem to imply that Defoe lived here or died here and perhaps even wrote *Robinson Crusoe* here. There is no record of any such thing, and no more than a faint possibility that he may have lodged here when he visited Bury in 1704 'in order to avoid the public gaze, and also to recuperate' after his ordeal in Newgate. It was, however, assuredly visited by Celia Fiennes, that extraordinary woman who rode side-saddle through England, reporting with odd punctuation and odder spelling on every feature of the land from stately mansions to bad inns. There is still plenty of scope for such a traveller.

The 'Nutshell' claims to be the smallest pub in Britain, and it is hard to imagine that any smaller one could stay in business. Its one diminutive bar is crammed with a confusion of relics: old guns, helmets, hatpins; packets of Victorian cigars and cigarettes with pretty names and the pictures of faded beauties; and, the latest addition to the miscellany of yesteryear, a potential antiquity—a five-shilling packet of halfpennies.

Bury was unhappily in the headlines several times from 1967 onwards, when troubles developed on a residential estate half a mile from the town centre. Deep holes opened up close to house-holders' front door steps, and sewers and gardens disappeared into greedy chasms. The building plot, once the property of the West Suffolk Hospital, was belatedly discovered to be situated immediately above some old chalk mine workings. Speleologists explored the network of tunnels and caves, and a protracted dispute began over the question of responsiblity. Other builders cautiously tested a further proposed development site and found another cavern in the summer of 1969, this time inexplicably roofed by a brick dome. It seems somewhat unjust that here, one of the few places with no romantic tradition of subterranean passages and chambers, and with no wish to concoct any such tradition, there should actually be such perils.

As a centre for exploration of inland Suffolk, Bury is incomparable. Roads radiate in every direction, testifying to the close connection which the town has had with its outlying villages from the days of monastic dominance through various agricultural and commercial phases up to the present status of county town. To the east, as we have discovered, is the Stowmarket road; west lies Newmarket. To the south there is a choice between Hadleigh via Lavenham, Sudbury via Appleton and Long Melford, and Haverhill through Chedburgh. Beside this latter road, where Out Westgate leaves the town, stands a memorial to the flamboyant Victorian novelist, Ouida.

Born on the first day of 1839 in Bury, she died and was buried in Italy in 1908. Her monument, erected by funds subscribed by readers of the *Daily Mirror* and bearing a message from the autocratic Curzon of Kedleston—surely one of the oddest of juxtapositions—consists of a column rising from a water trough. One of the mourning figures on the column holds a dog, but the trough was obviously for the use of horses. Today its water is filled with dead leaves and shreds of paper, and it is unlikely that any horse will venture this way: cars race past, brake, accelerate, roar off across the complexity of a five-road intersection, and facing the memorial across this tumult is a bright modern filling station.

Out of town to the north-west lies Hengrave Hall, an Elizabethan manor constructed not from the familiar fishtail red brick but from white brick and stone. It once had a moat, of which only a section remains. To inspect the interior, with its Tudor fireplaces, minstrels' gallery and panelling of different periods, permission must be obtained in advance from the Mother Superior of the sisterhood which since 1952 has used the Hall as a girls' school.

Once we are on this road, we are led on through Icklingham or through West Stow and the King's Forest into Breckland, one of the strangest areas in the whole of eastern England.

CHAPTER FIVE

Breckland to Broadland

More than a hundred Suffolk sites have disgorged valuable Roman remains, and it is impossible to estimate the number of individual caches of earlier archaeological treasures which the land has yielded up and continues to yield. Unfortunately, just as the salerooms of the county are now besieged by knowledgeable dealers bent on spiriting away its furniture, clocks and domestic heirlooms, so the historic and prehistoric villages and burial grounds are likely to be plundered by modern technicians. A new American ultra-sonic detector, on unrestricted sale to the general public, has been tested and has led the way to coins, Bronze Age jewellery, and other objects lying as much as six feet underground. More and more scheduled sites are being damaged by clumsy raiders, and there is a danger that sites as yet undiscovered will be rifled before expert teams can do their painstaking and ultimately more rewarding work.

No one region of the county can claim precedence in the richness of these crops. Bones and teeth of mammoth, bear, wild deer, wild cattle and horses were dug out of the mud beds of the ancient river under Stoke Hill, Ipswich, when the railway cutting and tunnel were being excavated; Mousterian implements have come from Mildenhall and the valley of the Gipping; flint instruments from earliest times turned up in a Hoxne brickyard at the end of the eighteenth century; bronze has gleamed out from Elveden, West-hall, Culford and a score of other localities. Benacre produced a leaden box heavy with nearly a thousand silver Roman coins; the British Museum houses a statue of Nero from Barking Hall.

Fragments of Romano-British pewter were found near Icklingham when Berner's Heath was being cleared in 1956 of explosives left on the firing ranges there. More recently, the Victorian vicarage attached to the local abandoned church came up for sale, and it was noticed that in the overgrown garden were two stone coffins. These proved to be of Roman origin. Forgotten since they were unearthed in 1871 by a labourer working for the vicar on land near the site of a Roman villa, they had originally been accompanied by a lead coffin which soon disappeared, probably to be melted down. Although there is no record of what happened to the stone coffins in the interim, it seems reasonable to suppose that the vicar took them into the grounds of his vicarage to use as rather ponderous ornamental containers for garden plants. There they remained, gradually succumbing to weeds and undergrowth, until their recent re-discovery.

Most splendid of all finds in this area was that of 1942, when a plough at West Row, near Mildenhall, jammed against something metallic and broke lose from its tractor. The farmer and ploughman dug out a collection of tableware which was at first thought to be pewter and not officially declared until 1946. It was then found to be fourth-century silver, and adjudged treasure trove. The Mildenhall Treasure is now in the British Museum, but replicas of some items are on display in Ipswich Museum, including the gleaming Oceanus dish showing the triumph of the wine-god Bacchus over drunken Hercules, in a swirl of dancing nereids, centaurs and satyrs. The items are not of local manufacture: they must have been imported from the Mediterranean, Gaul, and the East.

Mildenhall is not only a focus of some bygone age. It has links with a later county tradition, that of aviation. There were balloon ascents from Bury, Beccles and Ipswich in the 1780s, early research on flying boats and seaplanes at Felixstowe, pioneer radar work at Orford Ness and at Bawdsey; and from Mildenhall in 1934 Scott and Black took off for their famous win in the air race to Australia. Another winner associated with the town is a racehorse owned by Sir Thomas Charles Bunbury. In 1780 Sir Thomas, whose family were lords of the manor from 1747 to 1933, tossed a coin with Lord Derby to decide which of them should bestow his name upon a proposed annual race. He lost, so there is no annual Bunbury Day at Epsom; but as a consolation his Diomed won that first Derby.

Today the streets of Mildenhall are echo chambers for American aircraft landing and taking off. There are times when, claim the local inhabitants with a mixture of pride and ruefulness, traffic here is thicker than over London Airport. Yet the town has not been subdued or lost its eerily enchanting atmosphere. It has been here under this name since the Norman Conquest and is likely to remain here, stark and tenacious, at a junction of breck and fen. The parish is the largest in Suffolk and one of the largest in England. The market no longer has its old importance, but retains its hexagonal market cross from the time of Henry v, many times repaired and shored up, most recently in 1962.

Until 1895 the church was known as St Andrew's, but documents then came to light proving that it had originally been dedicated to St Mary, a name which has since been restored to it. It is an impressive building combining Early English, Decorated and Perpendicular styles. It has a huge north porch with vaulted ceiling and carved bosses. The angel roof of the nave is another of the truly angelic ones, and the aisles are looked down on by a multitude of Biblical figures, beasts, and heraldic devices. In 1930 parts of the woodwork were found to be pitted with small shot, and a couple of arrowheads were also found. Even Dowsing's minions were, mercifully, prevented by the soaring height of the roof from inflicting as much damage as usual.

The tower is a splendid mark for this part of the county and for Cambridgeshire beyond, as reliable as those coastal churches which provide seamarks for the mariner. It must have been awe-inspiring when topped with a spire, as it was until 1831.

Below it the large American cars, too large for the streets and lanes, come in for shopping or race through on their way to Bury, Thetford, or along the A.1101 which cuts across Mildenhall Fen until, in the view of we chauvinists, it runs right off the map. Here the fens are marked out with straight drains and spiky fences of trees little taller than hedges would have been, if there were any hedges. Whooping, shrieking gulls have flown this far inland to

27   *Southwold: East Green and lighthouse (1899)*

pursue tilting tractors across the heavy black earth. And darkness falls from the air: black fumes from the booming aeroplanes spray out above tractor and land like some sombre, drifting pesticide.

The barrows of Warren Hill, Roman camps and villas, Saxon settlements, all have as successors the airfields of the Second World War and airfields which remain to counter other possible threats. The thunder of planes above Mildenhall has not died before the note is taken up over Lakenheath, an American township of military buildings looking, from the road, like some vast holiday camp or a bright, aseptic industrial estate—a sort of murderous Bournville. There is a wide choice of traffic signs in the county, among them warnings against deer, black ice, racehorses, cattle, and even the soothing assurance of 'Toilets 6 miles'; but approaching Lakenheath we meet one which I find disquieting in a way I cannot, or perhaps do not wish to, explain: WARNING: CHILDREN AND TROOPS CROSSING.

Lord Kitchener, whose ancestors lived in Lakenheath, would possibly have appproved of all the military activity here. Before the boom of jets there was the rumble of tanks and guns, by no means silent yet. Elveden was the scene of the earliest tank training during the First World War, and across Breckland into Norfolk there are still large battle areas barred from the public by wire and notices threatening sudden death.

Breckland takes its name from the 'brecks' or 'brakes', tracts of heath and flint-strewn levels sporadically broken up for primitive cultivation but allowed to revert to wilderness. It provides the nearest approach in Britain to steppeland, its dry, sandy, easily blown soil the result of limestone and chalk particles washed out of boulder clay and glacial sands. In prehistoric times it was, as can be seen from its huge yield of tools, weapons, tumuli and other indications of extensive settlements, one of the most densely populated areas in the British Isles. Today it is one of the loneliest. The villages are sparse, tiny, and flinty. Its major town is Thetford, in Norfolk—but the county boundary here becomes rather nonsensical. The 200-300 square miles of the breck exist in themselves, remote from tidy administrative bodies.

28 *Walberswick: St Andrew's church seen over the river Blyth from Blackshore, Southwold*

Yet the contemporary features of this alien land have been moulded by a very powerful administrative body.

Game preserves occupied much of the region until the outbreak of the First World War. The only signs of civilization were the wooded parklands of the hunting gentry. The Dukes of Grafton had rights over great spreads of the terrain, kept their hounds at Euston and took them from place to place according to their plans for the hunt. One result of that war and its successor was an intensification of farming. But the most striking influence on the landscape has been that of the Forestry Commission.

Since its formation in 1919, the Commission has taken over large areas sold off to pay death duties and other taxes. Conifer forests have been planted in mathematical blocks, threatening eventually to darken the whole land between Swaffham and Bury. They are sinister to some, beautiful to others, but either way they have radically altered the whole character of the region. As a result of complaints on both ecological and aesthetic grounds, the Commission has slightly modified its policy and has for some time been introducing deciduous trees to break the monotony, especially by the roadside.

Older people regret the changes and miss much of the wild life which flourished here. But there is much left: the stone curlew and the wheatear have not fled; there are vetch, mallow, and heather like distant velvet. Sometimes between files of Scots pine the horizon is burnished with a promise of the sea just beyond. It is a delusion. There is something hallucinatory about most of Breckland. I fell under its spell many years ago, and am glad not to have been released from it yet.

The road from Mildenhall past Lakenheath, with Wangford Warren on our right subjugated now by trees instead of rabbits, leads into Brandon. It looks like an enlarged version of any of the scattered villages in this region: all flint; nothing decorative about the flint, just flint upon flint upon flint.

To trace a major source of this material we must cheat and cross the Ouse a mile into Norfolk. In a forest clearing is a switchback of dips and hummocks, 'Grime's Graves', its original purpose forgotten until the late nineteenth century. Historians theorized about ancient fortifications, British or Danish encampments. Then Canon William Greenwell began excavations to settle the matter, and discovered that the 'graves' were in fact flint mines from Neolithic times. In galleries 40 feet below the surface there remained deer antler picks which must have been laid aside just before a cave-in and never reclaimed. 'It was a most impressive sight', says the record of the digging, 'and one never to be forgotten to look, after a lapse of, it may well be, 3,000 years, upon a piece of work unfinished, with the tools of the workmen still lying where they had been placed so many centuries ago.'

The chalk formation from which flints can most easily be taken comes close to the surface in this area and in one freakish patch near Westleton, close to the coast. The lumps would be hauled to the surface and trimmed into axeheads and other implements.

From Neolithic times until the present day, Brandon has been the centre of this oldest of British industries. Quarried from pits on Lingheath Common long after Grime's Graves had been abandoned, flints have been cut and trimmed—or 'knapped'—here with tools differing in material but not essentially in form over the centuries. Brandon flints were said to have been the best in the world for use in firearms, and during the Napoleonic Wars the demand was so great that a large part of the local populace could rely on steady employment. Even until recent years there was a continuing demand from Africa, but now the supply has dwindled. A couple of craftsmen persevered in the yard behind the 'Flintknappers' Arms', but now regular production has ceased and only occasionally, more as a hobby than anything else, can the tap and squeak of the hammer be heard.

Brandon may also be remembered to posterity as the birthplace of Simon Eyre, the Lord Mayor of London who built Leadenhall and had what one might call a starring rôle in Dekker's *The Shoemaker's Holiday*.

On the outskirts of the town a branch off the B.1107 towards Thetford leads through woodland to Santon Downham, an idyllic riverside village housing the headquarters of the Forestry Commission and many of its employees. In 1668 a strong south-west wind blew great tides of sand from the warrens into Santon Downham and came nigh to drowning it. Furze hedges were planted and high banks were built to bind and control the land, but it seemed almost impossible to make a stable, fertile area of it. Today it is drenched in greenery of every hue.

The Commission has laid out a two-mile forest trail, starting from and winding back to the car park beside its headquarters. Seats are provided at reasonable intervals. The walk makes its way agreeably through an 1880 plantation of elm, beech, chestnut and oak, followed by a Corsican pine and oak plantation laid out by schools, parish councils, the United States Air Force and distinguished visitors to commemorate the jubilee of the Commission's birth. One of the most glowing sights on a sunny day is the lime avenue, part of the forest trail and also an accompaniment to the road out in the Thetford direction. The original trees were planted in 1880, the most recent additions being in 1965. About 90 yards are felled and replanted every 10 years to maintain the avenue in its present lovely condition.

To avoid plunging into Norfolk once and for all, we must retrace our steps and take the road from Brandon to Elveden, alternately gloomed at and smiled at by the bright-dark flicker of the enclosing forest.

Elveden Hall's Oriental extravagance was prompted by its then owner, the Maharajah Duleep Singh, in 1870, and later carried further for the Earl of Iveagh when a pastiche Taj Mahal was added. Duleep Singh did much for East Anglia, including the donation of the Ancient House in Thetford as a Breckland museum, but his greatest delight seems to have been found in the slaughter of game: he was proud of having managed to shoot nearly 800 partridge during one day in 1876.

A short distance along the A.11 towards Mildenhall, a tall Corinthian column dwarfs the conifer guardsmen closing in on it. A war memorial to men of the three parishes of Elveden, Briswell and Icklingham, which meet here, it has an internal staircase which once

gave access to the top, like that of the Monument in London, but this has now been shut off.

Another route from the Elveden crossroads leads back to Bury through the King's Forest, past a good roadside picnic place provided by the Forestry Commission, and a forest trail not too arduous for the leisurely walker. Before reaching Bury there is a turn-off to Ingham and the pretty cluster of Ampton, from which a long mere curls towards Great Livermere. The rectory here was the home of M. R. James for 44 years. He records the derivation of the name as being from *læfer*, a flag, which grows with bulrushes around the mere. James lamented changes in the locality during his own time, and there must have been others since, but 'village and park have some beauty left', he said then, and this is still true.

Now we are caught up in another proliferation of by-roads which offer the chance of discovering places or moods which may not have been caught by the gazetteers and guidebooks. Every man for himself—but at this point I recommend a swing back north to Barnham and then along the wooded road into Euston, bright-faced and unfailingly smart along its village street. There are only about 200 inhabitants, including some old people in the trim memorial cottages near the park gates. The church of St Genevieve is within the park, as was most of the village itself before being remodelled outside the gates in the seventeenth century.

Euston Hall standing in a 1,200-acre park planted by William Kent in the middle of the eighteenth century and resplendent with oak and cedar, was itself built in the time of Charles II but suffered from a fire in 1902, and was reduced to its present form in 1951. The Little Ouse flows through the estate, crossed by an ornamental bridge, and through the trees from the road one catches tantalizing glimpses of a pseudo-Greek temple which was originally meant as a banqueting hall.

There is a pleasant road to Rushford, but while in this neighbourhood we ought to pay a respectful nod to Honington, the birthplace of Robert Bloomfield. The last of six children, he was born in 1766 and, with the other five, brought up by his widowed mother who kept a dame's school in their cramped wattle-and-daub cottage.

She married again before he was seven, and from then on he was left to acquire such knowledge as he could on his own, apart from a few writing lessons from a schoolmaster in Ixworth. He worked on a farm on the Euston estate, from which he gained most of the inspiration for his bucolic poem, *The Farmer's Boy*, written when he was in London but redolent of the world around Honington. Its success in London and in foreign translation enabled him to revisit Suffolk, and the county continued to provide him with all the themes he needed. The Duke of Grafton helped him by securing him a post in the Stamp Office, but in spite of this and his brief, heady fame he died a pauper.

One should wander receptively rather than purposefully through Coney Weston, Barningham and Hopton to Redgrave. Overlooking the wide lake there once stood the home of Sir Nicholas Bacon, Lord Keeper to Queen Elizabeth I, later to be taken over and rebuilt by the Holt family. Both Bacon and Sir John Holt, the great lawyer and Chief Justice, are buried in the church.

Near Redgrave are the sources of both the boundary rivers, the Little Ouse and the Waveney. Tracing the course of the gentle, meandering Waveney from here to its meeting with the Yare on Breydon Water is as good a way of passing a week of one's life as any I can imagine. Two or three extra weeks will sharpen the palate rather than dull it.

All along the valley the stumps of round church towers jut up—Stuston, Brome, Syleham, Barsham, on to Herringfleet—like a straggling army of dragon's teeth protecting the peaceful meadows and marshy fringes. Most massive of them all is that of Wortham, now empty and disintegrating, yet looking as though it may have a few defiant centuries left. A vast weed-choked shell built against the church but not integrated with it, it is 60 feet high and 30 feet in diameter, with walls four feet thick. On its rim it balances a diminutive wooden belfry like some disproportionate dovecot.

The rector of Wortham from 1825 to 1877 was Richard Cobbold, whose name will always be associated with a distant part of the county. Perhaps it was his nostalgia for the banks and marshes of another river, the Orwell, that led him to write with such romantic abandon the novel, *Margaret Catchpole*. We shall meet the misguided girl again when we reach the inlets and moorings where she fell in love and into misfortune.

At a junction of lanes above the church, on the way in from Redgrave, is a squat pillar bearing a plaque which might puzzle the visitor whose knowledge of recent history is pitted with as many gaps as my own. It reads:

THE TITHE WAR

———

134 PIGS AND 15 CATTLE
(VALUE £702)
SIEZED FOR TITHE
FEB. 22ND. 1934

This commemorates the distraint of livestock from Mr and Mrs Rash of the nearby Manor House, which, in spite of an impressive platoon of yew sentinels, had no effective defence against the Church of England in pursuit of its traditional levies. Mrs Rash, better known as the novelist Doreen Wallace, wrote a splendidly vigorous book—now unfortunately out of print—about this agricultural battle before it reached what neither side could reasonably call victory.

During the depression of the 1920s and 1930s, farmers were still expected to pay tithes on a revalued rate which assessed every pre-war £100 at £105, plus another £4. 10s towards a sinking fund against the day when tithes should be abolished—which they showed no sign of being. But the price of corn, on which these assessments were in theory largely based, had slumped disastrously. Farmers could not afford to pay and did not see why they, unlike business-men, factory owners and shopkeepers, should in fact have to continue maintaining a Church of which no more than 10 per cent of them were practising members.

The collection of tithes, originally in the hands of individual parsons, was by now a function of the commissioners of Queen Anne's Bounty. When farmers proved uncooperative, these authorities sent in hauliers to carry away livestock and produce in lieu of the money owed. Local auctioneers began by selling off such seizures at absurd nominal prices to friendly farmers who then returned the animals to their original owners. Soon it was ordered that the sales figures had to meet the tithe sum due. Local markets grew more and more reluctant to handle such goods, and attempts were made to sell further afield. Dealers all over the country grew wary of stock which might be tithe goods. On one occasion a load of cattle and pigs was rushed by train from East Anglia to Crewe in the hope of disposing of it before buyers in that area were alerted; but a local motor-cyclist set off across country and reached the market ahead of the goods, effectively disrupting the sale.

With the connivance of Queen Anne's Bounty, a firm called General Dealers was set up, prepared to tender for 'distressed' chattels and to carry out their removal. Because local hauliers wanted no part in this distasteful business, lorries now came from as far away as Durham and Northumberland, escorted by police and loaded with hired roughnecks—'bailiff's officers', in official language—to raid the farms of Suffolk and Norfolk.

Roads and entrances to farms were accidentally blocked with remarkable frequency. Tractors and hay balers had a habit of breaking down across gateways. Drainage trenches just happened to be in course of construction when the forces of law (law rather than justice) arrived.

The seizures went on. In one case planks were laid across a trench and pigs were cruelly lifted by ears and tail to be dumped into improvized sedan chairs, carted over the bridge, and tossed into the waiting vans. 'If *we'd* handled any of our animals that way', said one incensed farmer, 'we'd have had the R.S.P.C.A. and police down on us right away.' Yet here were the police actually protecting such louts!

A broadsheet parody of Lewis Carroll was widely circulated under the title *The Bounty and the Bailiff*. Its final stanza runs:

'O Farmers,' said the Bailiff,
'You've had a pleasant run!'
'Shall we be trotting home again?'
But answer was there none—
And this was scarcely odd because
They'd sold up every one.

Having refused outright to set up a Royal Commission to study the injustice of tithe law, the Prime Minister, Stanley Baldwin, eventually did set one up, soon after a large London demonstration by tithepayers. In 1936 a new Act was passed. It agreed that tithes should be gradually phased out, but against the advice of the Commission it allowed a period of 60 years over which this run-down should stretch. It also agreed that the overall valuation should work out at 17 per cent less than that which was currently being claimed.

As a *quid pro quo*, a nasty little clause was written in to allow the treatment of tithe redemption arrears as a personal debt, so that not merely farm stock and produce but personal possessions could be distrained, and the tithepayer could even be made bankrupt.

Still dissatisfied with the situation, the dauntless Doreen Wallace and her husband decided to stage a test case and obtain as much useful publicity as possible. Having withheld payment, they watched the authorities remove furniture from the house and auction it in a marquee on the lawn. Members of the Tithepayers' Association rallied round and bought various items until the sum required was attained. The furniture was then carried back into the house. That evening an effigy of Queen Anne was ceremoniously burned on a bonfire.

Another memorial to martyrs of those quarrelsome days is to be found at Elmsett, near Hadleigh.

This civil war might have intensified had not a larger war come along. It became more important to fight Hitler than to harass the British Government. By the time the Second World War ended, farmers were doing very well indeed and have continued to prosper until these last few years. The collection of tithe redemption payments is now in the hands of the Inland Revenue, and for many farmers it slips through along with other taxes without their really noticing that they, and they alone, are supporting the supposedly national Established Church.

Quite recently Mr A. G. Mobbs of Oulton discovered that the Inland Revenue records of the land on which he is paying off his dues were based on statistics 130 years old and include property which he has never even owned or which he disposed of long ago. He is now applying for a rebate covering the whole period. Furthermore, Mr Mobbs has extracted from the House of Lords a copy of a shelved Bill whose terms, he says, 'prove conclusively that agriculture is not the only industry liable to tithe payments'—among others, Members of Parliament are liable.

It is indeed a blissful thought. Is it too much to hope that Income Tax inspectors, too, are subject to tithe?

The nearest town of any size is busy, bustling Diss. But Diss is in Norfolk, and a bit of a raider: it long ago stole the market from declining Eye. Approaching Eye from any direction, one feels it will prove to be a town of some consequence. It is particularly impressive from the Hoxne road, which curves below the stalwart church and then climbs steeply past the stump of the castle on the right and the large houses on either side. The marketplace, when reached, is a sad disillusionment. Something is lacking. In 1946 Leonard Thompson could write: 'But for the fact that its interesting number of picturesque, little, old houses are all clean and fresh-looking, the empty streets would almost suggest a town from which the inhabitants have fled overnight.' There has been no noticeable revival between that day and this.

In the eighteenth century Eye knew some prosperity from the manufacture of lace, now forgotten. In the following century it had a mill, now gone. Diss has its market.

The 'White Lion' hotel fortunately survives as a focus for local activities and meetings. Flanking one side of its old stable yard is an attractive barn of a ballroom with a musician's gallery. Ornamental vents in the ceiling could once be operated by long poles when it became desirable to allow smoke to escape into the loft. They have since been foolishly sealed over with paint, so that the atmosphere tends to grow thick and choking—especially on those Thursdays when the place resounds incongruously to Trad Jazz.

It would be pleasant if functions could be as jolly and inexpensive as they were over a hundred years ago, when the *Suffolk Chronicle* recorded a review of the County Yeomanry. 'After the Inspection, which proved a fine treat to all admirers of the art of warfare and agriculture united in the same individuals, a retreat was made to the "White Lion" where dinner was provided at 2s 6d a head, including as much wine and punch as each man could swallow.'

A tributary of the Waveney, the river Dove, flows through a nearby village of cosy charm, another of those with a tilted triangular green topped by its church. It is prettier than many a more photographed place, but is remembered not for this prettiness but for a grim page in East Anglian history. At Hoxne (pronounced Hoxen) tradition has it that King Edmund died, a tradition so strong that no doubts cast by some eminent scholars have caused any significant amendment to the original story. It was recorded that he met his death at Heglisdune: this, assert some, was corrupted into Hoxne; others deride the notion and favour the idea of Suthtune, nearer the coast—now Shottisham. Legend, with many accretions, insists that it was Hoxne.

Edmund is believed to have fled in this direction after the rout of his army at Barnham. The Danes were dangerously close when the King took shelter under what was later to be known as the Bridge of the Golden Spurs. He was betrayed by a wedding party crossing the bridge. There are two versions of this episode. One makes the betrayal an unlucky chance: as the Danes stood back to allow the revellers to pass (uncharacteristically courteous of them, in the light of their general behaviour at the time), one man saw the gleam of the royal spurs reflected in the stream. The other story blames the bride herself: seeing Edmund, and knowing that the Danes were offering a reward for his capture, she pointed him out and collected the money to add to her dowry. When he was dragged out, Edmund laid a curse on the bridge and on every bride and groom who should cross it on their wedding day. Nobody can tell whether the curse still operates: to this day no girl will go to her wedding over Goldbrook Bridge.

Captured, King Edmund was abjured to recant his Christian beliefs and swear loyalty to the Danish Ingvar and his gods. Edmund refused. He was then bound to an oak tree so that soldiers could shoot arrows into him, after which he was beheaded.

When his followers came to reclaim the body and, with the miraculous intervention of the wolf, to find his head, they laid the remains in the chapel of a Benedictine monastery on whose site now stands Abbey Farm. A memorial marks the spot where an oak tree fell in 1848, revealing a Danish arrowhead embedded in the trunk in confirmation of the stubborn local belief that this was indeed the tree against which the King was slain. Timber from it was used to make the Victorian screen in the church.

On a windy plateau to the east, what appears at first to be the ochre wall of a manor house glimmers between the trees. It proves to be one side of a moated castle, the only inhabited castle left in the county, its frontage resplendent with turrets and battlements. There is in fact little behind the gatehouse and that noble wall apart from gardens and the manor house to one side, but Wingfield Castle makes a fine flourish on this otherwise desolate expanse. The village of Wingfield shelters in a hollow, its large church humped above a tight twist of narrow roads. Within the church are the tombs of the de la Poles, including the first Duke of Suffolk, who married Chaucer's granddaughter, and tombs of the family which gives the place its name: Sir John Wingfield, one of the Black Prince's knights, founded a college here, now superseded by a farmhouse.

Mention of Fressingfield seems to generate two almost Pavlovian reactions from those who know the area. The gourmet happily recalls the adventurous cuisine of the 'Fox and Goose', an inn which was once a guildhall close against the churchyard, its standards consistently high under changing managements. The explorer of old churches says 'bench ends'. It would be nice to find something strikingly original to say; but why seek diligently for novelty when the old truths remain true? It may seem strange to describe carvings of the emblems of the Passion and of saintly devices as boisterous, but there is something so assured and joyful in the execution of these designs that I can think of no more appropriate description.

William Sancroft of Ufford Hall is buried in a tomb, with an epitaph chosen by himself, close to the flint-panelled south porch. He was Dean of St Paul's and then Archbishop of Canterbury. He crowned King James II, but found himself forced to defend the Anglican Church against James's wiles, and with six loyal bishops successfully countered a charge of seditious libel brought by the King, with a resulting outburst of jubilant 'bells and bonfires all over England'. His conscience caused him further anguish when he found himself unable to take the oath to William and Mary, and he returned to Fressingfield, where he died in 1693.

Beyond is the flatness of Metfield, where grass, bracken and stunted bushes have gouged their way through the remaining slabs of the old airfield. The village is nothing; yet I recall turning the corner a year or two ago and coming upon a wealth of apple blossom on the one tree drooping over the little puddle of a village pond, and it remains one of those sudden, immediately recorded pictures that stay bright in the mind long after more imposing views have been blurred or forgotten.

It needs only a few miles to take us back to the richer valley of the Waveney, with Mendham amiable on its shallow slope. Sir Alfred Munnings, most boisterous and contumacious of the painters of this past century, was born here and made many of his early horse paintings here. Any older inhabitant will be only too delighted to point out the field in which he kept his caravan and to tell stories, most of them so outrageous as to be utterly convincing, of his exploits and of his bellowed, often bawdy, ballads. Like another East Anglian, George Borrow, he was greatly enamoured of the gipsies and their way of life, and probably had more pleasure as a young man trailing round with them and painting their animals than as the honoured, feared and often deplored President of the Royal Academy he later became.

We are now on the fringe of 'the Saints'. This wide scattering of tiny hamlets includes St Peter, St Michael, All Saints and St Nicholas, St Lawrence, and, confusingly, two St Margarets. One of them recently complained of a neglect so dire that its name did not appear on any local signpost, even on the upright at its own road junction. Homersfield was once included in the holy band as South Elmham St Mary. The present South Elmham Hall occupies the site of a Norman palace built by the then Bishop of Norwich, founder of Norwich Cathedral.

Off the road between St James and St Cross lies a rarely visited minster of the seventh century. Today, choked by undergrowth, there remain fragments of the tower and nave only, though clearly there was also a chancel. It seems most likely that this was the collegiate centre of a group of evangelizing priests. They must often have felt as cold and lost as the Roman occupation forces or, later, the airmen on these infinite fields. At least, though, the airmen had speedy transport to the market and shopping towns of Halesworth and Bungay.

Halesworth we have already visited. Bungay has a lot more to offer.

The very name of the town amuses and puzzles visitors. Its onomatopaeic jollity sings very well in the title of H. G. Wells' *Tono Bungay*, a novel about a marvellous patent elixir. There are various theories to account for its origin. Some trace a derivation from Bongué, 'good ford', and certainly this has always been one of the important crossings of the Waveney—whose water meadows, it may be added, flood here with alarming regularity. A Victorian philologist established the existence of a family of Angles called Bonning who settled here and also gave their name to Boninghall, in Kent, one in Shropshire, and one in Buckinghamshire. Yet another writer says that the tip of land on which the town has grown up, protruding so far into the Waveney as to cause it to change course, was known in the distant past as Le bon Eye, later corrupted to Bongeye and then Bungay.

Exact dates of buildings and events before 1688 are hard to establish, as in that year a fire destroyed most of the town and its records. The flames which gutted much of St Mary's church and weakened the tower were so fierce as to melt the bells. The whole of the marketplace was obliterated, and eyewitnesses counted no more than five or six houses left standing. Rumour had it that the outbreak was the work of Papists, and for long afterwards the description 'As great a rogue as burnt Bungay' was a common local insult.

After reconstruction the town struggled back to life and soon boasted its own theatre in the Castle Yard, and a Gentleman's Club. A few survivors complained, as people will, that the new Bungay could not compare with the old. The new St Mary's church was said to be unsafe, the new buildings were no match for those which had gone, and so many original residents and tradesmen had departed with their families that it had become in effect a settlement of newcomers.

The town sign portrays the castle and a black dog, stabbed by forked lightning. The animal is said to represent the Devil, but has a family resemblance to the dreaded Black Shuck. This creature appears in one guise and another all over Suffolk. Near the coast he is a hellhound whose howling through a gale presages disaster and who has been accused of dragging children out to sea. In Breckland he is an unidentifiable beast with flaming eyes. At Bungay on one occasion he was more fearsomely direct than anywhere, rushing in broad daylight into the church and tearing out the throats of some worshippers. Like so many apparitions, he proved useful not only to mothers eager to terrorize their children but also to smugglers who preferred folk to stay indoors at certain hours: it was simple enough to hang a lantern round the neck of a large dog or pony and guide it through the darkness along a route which it was intended to keep clear for the night's work. Bungay is now a fair distance from the coast, but in its heyday it shared a brisk smuggling activity with Beccles.

It is hardly surprising that there have been tales of Bigod ghosts haunting the castle ruins: vexatious in life, the family would surely not have been expected to rest easy after death.

Bungay Castle was built in Stephen's time, most probably without his overt permission. When he crushed Bigod's rebellion and ordered the demolition of Framlingham, Bungay was also taken but not utterly destroyed. It was not until the Leicester insurrection that it was razed to the ground. Permission was given by Edward 1 to Roger Bigod for rebuilding, and the fragments which remain are from that period.

After Roger's death the castle was neglected until it became 'old and ruinous and worth nothing a year'. In 1766 the owner was a Mr Mickleborough, who tried to break up the walls so that he could sell the stones for road-mending but found the flint and lime construction so sturdy that he had to desist. He sold off the ruins to Elizabeth Bonhote, a novelist whose husband was a solicitor and a captain in the Second Company of the Bungay Volunteers. She equipped the keep as a summer residence, thriftily recouped her expenses by using the background for a novel called *Bungay Castle*, and finally disposed of it to the then Duke of Norfolk, who was anxious to have it back in the family.

Today the 'White Lion' stands over the foundations of what must once have been part of extensive fortifications. Fragments of old wall jut out into alleys and across paths like raggedly chopped hunks of toffee-and-nut brittle. Traces of a subterranean passage were discovered years ago, and some depressions in Castle Yard have been identified as fishponds.

In spite of the parochialism and mistrust of newcomers shown by survivors of the fire, Bungay can claim to have attracted and made welcome many distinguished visitors. Hannah More, finding the town better than she had been led to expect, 'very clean and pleasant ... the good folks have no bad taste', approved also of its cultural standards and assured Garrick that he was much admired here. Chateaubriand lived in Bridge Street for some years during his exile from France after the Terror had threatened to engulf him, eking out a living by teaching French privately in a room here and at Beccles College. Rider Haggard mentions a local reference to him as 'Monsieur Shatterbrain'. Agnes Strickland came to visit her sister, who had married into the Childs family—a family which was to leave a significant mark upon the community. John Childs, who kept open house for writers and celebrities, established a private printing works here: it gave employment then to many people in the town, and still does so under the well-known name of Richard Clay.

One temporary resident did not take so kindly to Bungay. George Crabbe attended Mr Harvey's school and hated it. Discipline was harsh, not to say sadistic. Echoes of Crabbe's misery linger on in passages of *The Borough*. The unhappy boy was relieved to be transferred from what was obviously an early example of a crudely materialistic commercial college to a school at Stowmarket where more attention was paid to the classics.

Today the old market cross remains in worthy condition, set back from a road junction whose conflicting traffic lanes, lines, arrows and dashes are untranslatable even by one who has been through the town a score of times. It is crowned by a statuette of Justice, and once sheltered a cage in which malefactors were exposed to the taunts of the public. Justice, however, could be tempered by mercy, or perhaps by cash: the landlord of the 'Swan' was prepared, for a consideration, to provide alternative accommodation in one of his rooms whose bedstead was fitted with shackles.

There are some fine red-brick houses on the Trinity side of St Mary's churchyard, and elsewhere many upper storeys worthy of attention, though some roofs and gables have been half obscured by a medley of frontages and extensions stuck on like cardboard.

St Mary's itself looks oddly foreshortened because of its lack of a chancel. There were plans at one time to build a chancel which would incorporate the priory ruins at present abutting the east end, but nothing came of them. The main entrance is through the north porch, which was once used in fine weather as a school; in winter the children had lessons in the chamber above. In the churchyard near the porch is the Bungay Stone, some three feet high and reputed to be about 2,000 years old. Until recent times there was a children's ritual of dancing round it twelve times and pretending to invoke the Devil. This and other local superstitions link the stone with ancient Druidic rites. It seems to share many attributes with a Witch's Stone at Westleton, which boys and girls also circled in a breathless game.

Holy Trinity is far older than St Mary's, and although damaged by the fire has retained some of its basic structure. The north wall dates from about 1000, the round tower from some 40 years later. The east window's gable arch confirms the Saxon origin of the building.

The road to Bungay's most distinguished neighbour runs through Barsham, whose round tower is 'the most perfect to the eye' in the opinion of the late Julian Tennyson, contrasting it unfavourably with 'the most gaunt and uncouth' monster of Wortham. Roos Hall is a glowing brick manor house of the sixteenth century, with fine turrets and chimneys. Nelson's mother was born in the rectory.

But there is no road approach to Beccles which can match the waterway. Here the Waveney is at its most ravishing. In summer there may be a traffic jam of pleasure craft, but before the holiday-makers come, or after they have gone—and it would be an ill-tempered critic who resented their good taste in choosing such a setting for a holiday—the traveller who is in no hurry and does not mind a cool breeze gossiping across the stream from the reeds will find rare delights here. I have come downstream on a November morning when the stillness of the air enjoined stillness upon every last detail, so that my memory now holds it clear and unbreakable. Leafless branches are sketched in filigree on the sullen yet luminous sky, each thread of twig faithfully reflected in the water. We drift for a while, sky and water become interchangeable like a trick picture, reality and reflection the same, the mirrored world upside-down ... or are *we* upside-down? Across the marshes, mobile grabs like metal giraffes are eating not from the trees but from the ground, grubbing up earth and sipping mud from the edge of a ditch. Even their intermittent coughing and clanking are subdued, unresonant, in the stillness.

As we turn that last bend in the river, Beccles church tower is framed between the brittle webs of the trees. It becomes a pivot, edging unpredictably off centre as we follow the convoluted waterway, then thrusting up dead ahead once more. Gradually the red Georgian backbone of the town stiffens itself out of green marsh and meadow, lightened here and there by a splash of Suffolk pink like a carelessly dropped blob of strawberry ice-cream. Gardens slope down to the water, bedecked with decrepit huts and boat-houses. There are slime-green landings, waterlogged boats, sleek boats, smart moorings and crumbling steps. The tower of St Michael's dips slightly now, blunt between the houses, squat above the rooftops.

Many of the luckier houses in Beccles turn their backs on the town, the better to contemplate river and marsh. In spite of this and in spite of the one-way rush of traffic towards Norwich and Yarmouth, Northgate retains its dignity with its elegant doorways, Dutch gables, glimpses of the Waveney and glimpses of garden in a happy blend. Higher up, on the approach from Bungay, Bally-gate (the old Baileygate) offers an alluring view across to Norfolk.

The centre of the town is an untidy square dominated by that bell tower which has been beckoning us in from such a distance. Standing apart from the church, it is 92 feet high. Construction began in the fifteenth century but was never completed. The mighty south porch has the dimensions of a castle gatehouse, with windows in its upper chamber, a turret staircase, and corner pinnacles. Above the arch are the familiar crowns transfixed by arrows. In 1749 Catherine Suckling came from Barsham to wed the Reverend Edward Nelson in this church. Nine years later she gave birth to an Horatio Nelson who survived, an earlier son of that name having died in infancy. In 1783 George Crabbe at last married his long-desired Sarah Elmy here.

As with Bungay, there has been a long smuggling tradition. In the days when a large area of Broadland was still a wide estuary and waves reached the foot of the low cliff on which Beccles is built, this was a major herring fishery port. Now there remain only the narrowing river and the busy yacht station with its trim greens, rattling shrouds, and the chug and stutter of engines. Then there was a busy movement of contraband, and from one house alone were several well-worn tracks across the countryside to facilitate delivery and distribution.

Some routes linked up with Oulton, and activities there may well have had something to do with the supposed haunting of High House. This originally belonged to the Fastolf family, kinsmen of the unforgettable Sir John Falstaff, who gave lavishly to Oulton church. Brasses of Sir John Fastolf, who died in 1445, and his wife Katherine were once set near the chancel door, but now only the matrices in the floor show their dimensions. There are two contradictory versions of the supposed haunting of the hall. One tells of a squire who murdered his wife in the room beside the front door and was thereafter condemned to ride repeatedly up to and into the house on a coal-black horse with ravening hounds foaming at his heels; the other of the wife poisoning the squire and being condemned to walk every night at midnight, forever holding the poison cup before her as she went. Doubtless during the many years when it was shut and uninhabited the hall could have been a useful warehouse, and the phantom or phantoms most trustworthy guardians.

The pride of the interior was its rich panelling, but earlier this century a Lowestoft antique dealer who had bought the premises removed all this and shipped it to a buyer in the United States.

Oulton Broad is the only spacious section of Broadland in Suffolk, a mile long and with an average width of half a mile. Craft of every kind moor here, boats are built and repaired along its banks all year round, and during the season there is motor boat racing. Conducted tours start from here, but spend most of their allotted time on river and reedy channel: the Broads proper are some miles to the north.

When George Borrow married the widowed Mary Clarke, who had persevered in her intention of capturing him and at last succeeded, he came into possession of Oulton Hall and the summerhouse overlooking the Broad where he was to spend most of the remaining years of his life. Having made friends with the East Anglian gipsies, he gave them permission to camp at any time on part of his estate near St Michael's church. This did not please Sir Morton Peto of Somerleyton Hall, who was perpetually at loggerheads with Borrow. When Peto bought the right to take his railway from Lowestoft to Reedham across part of Borrow's land, he boasted that the profit made from gravel removed during the operation more than covered the cost of the permission. Borrow raged against him, accused him to his face of being a highwayman, and left a picture of him to posterity in the shape of Mr Flamson Flaming in *The Romany Rye*, written here during 1856.

Some guidebooks call Somerleyton Hall 'handsome'. For my own part I can imagine it at ease only beside a Wirral golf course, where it might display a certain grotesque grandeur among all those Ruabon brick turrets. Conceived in the sixteenth century, it was altered in 1844 according to Peto's tastes—'a pandemonium in red brick', according to his old enemy. The contents are noteworthy, however: pictures, tapestries and some Grinling Gibbons carving. The public are admitted on Sunday, Thursday and Bank Holiday Monday afternoons from Easter to September. Far and away the most attractive features are the ornamental gardens and shrubberies, and there is an amusing maze.

Peto managed to transform the entire village, leaving us with a collection of sugary, embellished cottages and school. In 1847 the Lowestoft Harbour and Railway Company dutifully aped its master's style when building the railway station. This hilarious penchant to the Hall, complete with coat of arms and an absurd chimney, is now an unstaffed halt and the building itself has been sold off as a private residence. Platforms look out over the marshes and the river, which the railway crosses by a resonant iron swing bridge, with Herringfleet mill standing to one side like some esoteric signalling apparatus. In the past it may have been just this: the sails of many such drainage mills were used to convey messages and warnings to smugglers operating across the flats.

The operation of Herringfleet smock mill, preserved in working order by East Suffolk County Council, must have been extremely cumbersome. The sails are designed to carry cloths which have to be laboriously fixed by hand, trimmed to suit the prevailing wind.

The county here thrusts out a promontory akin to the Newmarket spur and the jagged scoop west of Thetford. Norfolk runs down the far side of the looping Waveney and crowds in from Yarmouth on the east. The A.143 is carried into Suffolk across the river by an iron suspension bridge, close to the excavated shreds of St Olave's priory. This Augustinian foundation is the last surviving commemoration of the Norse saint since another St Olave near Needham Market was swallowed up by Creeting St Mary. The priory bakehouse and brewhouse have been incorporated into an adjacent farm. There is some rare fourteenth-century brick vaulting.

The A.143 continues past Fritton Decoy, sheltered by trees and connected to the complicated waterways of river and Broadland only by a channel not negotiable by boats. Three miles long, curving gently through its woodland, it is well stocked with fish, and fishing is allowed between June and September. There are rowing boats for hire. It would be hard to find a more tranquil stretch of water on which to spend a soothing afternoon. The only disturbances are caused by skimming, splashing, voluble wildfowl. The decoy itself is a semicircular network tunnel leading into a netted trap. Tame ducks lure their wilder cousins into this tunnel, through which they are driven into the snare.

Overlooking a widening reach where the Waveney and the Yare flow into Breydon Water is Burgh Castle. A marina has been developed nearby with shop, bar, caravan site, moorings and slipway. The ancient ruin is more easily reached from here than from the village: lured on by the promise of the Ancient Monument signposts along the inland lanes, the driver assumes he will soon be able to get to the castle, only to find that it stands on private farmland at the end of a rutted track which can often become a quagmire.

Like Beccles, but long before Beccles existed as such, Burgh Castle was lapped by the waters of what was then an estuary. Its Roman name, Gariannonum, has an obvious linguistic affinity with the river Yare. The Romans established it as a fort of the Saxon Shore to ward off possible attacks from the Iceni and to serve as a supply port for galleys bringing men, arms and provisions. In its original form the castle was rectangular and enclosed about six acres. Only three walls of mortar-bound rubble, 15 feet high and five feet thick at the top, 11 feet at the base, with a facing of flint and tiles, now remain; the western wall collapsed down the slope. The corners are rounded and protected by towers, and there are other towers at intervals along the walls. At the top of one tower wall is a space which must have accommodated the turntable of some military engine.

This was almost certainly the fortress called Cnobheresbury given by King Sigebert to the Irish missionary St Fursay when he came in

633 to win converts among the East Angles, and when, according to Bede. 'By the example of his virtue, and the efficacy of his discourse, he converted many unbelievers to Christ, and confirmed by his faith and love those that already believed.' In this bleak spot St Fursay had many trances and visions.

After the Norman Conquest the walls were used as the bailey of a castle. Then, as now, it must have been a windy spot—exhilarating or frightening, most suitably a place in which to have visions.

If we are to stay in Suffolk we must now turn back. There is little elbow-room. This sense of being squeezed in is symbolized by Blundeston church, with the leanest round tower of them all.

The church is in part Norman, but this oddly tapering tower is probably Saxon. The bench ends are a riot of poppyheads. Its porch sundial has been immortalized by *David Copperfield*, glowing anew every morning in the eyes of young David, born and bred in the neighbouring Rookery. It was from here that Barkis would take him to the delights of Yarmouth and the friendship of Peggotty.

When the 1969 version of Dickens' novel was made for showing in British cinemas and on American television, authentic locations were sought; but some had to be changed. Yarmouth could not play the part of Yarmouth: there was almost nothing left of the old town and shore; the background was that of a gaudy modern holiday resort. In the end Peggotty's boat was set on the shore near Benacre Broad, and Southwold was chosen as the town: it had altered less than any of the other coastal towns, and once television aerials had been temporarily removed and the modern pillar-box and concrete lamp standard suitably masked, it provided an impeccable setting.

The name of 'Blunderstone', which is how Dickens misread it on a signpost, presented itself to him while he was walking from Yarmouth to Lowestoft. In a letter he described Lowestoft as 'a fine place'. When so many places have changed, while others remain unspoilt, how stands Lowestoft today? We are close enough, now, to see for ourselves.

CHAPTER SIX

Easternmost England

In a letter published in the local newspaper early in 1970 a Lowestoft resident wrote of 'the social retardment of the town' and complained that not merely was it necessary to go to Yarmouth for any kind of entertainment but that one even had to go there to be cremated. 'But', he added, 'we have a cemetery—it covers the entire borough.'

This gloomy view of the second largest town in the county recalls the similar distaste of Thomas Nashe, born here in 1567. This sardonic, roistering, extravagant poet, friend of Green and Marlowe, also found Yarmouth more desirable and wrote warmly of it, 'Because I had money lent me at Yarmouth and I pay them again praise of their own town and the red herring.'

I confess that I find Lowestoft drab and inhospitable, its back streets like those of a north-country slum without the northern vitality, its vauntedly 'picturesque' Scores about as picturesque as the equally steep back alleys of a Welsh mining town, and its congested traffic quite appalling. The traffic problem is made worse by the unreliability of the swing bridge across the harbour, the narrowest and nastiest hazard on the whole of the A.12. This bridge is in process of being replaced, but access from either side cannot be greatly improved, and nobody in the district supposes that any miracle is about to be worked.

Yet every year holidaymakers crowd gladly into the town. They certainly cannot find any of that elegance referred to in Edwardian days and even up to the beginning of the last war. There must be something bracing in the air—this is, after all, the easternmost tip of the British Isles—and other charms which Nashe, the newspaper correspondent and I have missed.

There is no doubting the dogged courage of Lowestoft's history. In the time of Henry VIII, 14 ships were engaged in cod fishing in Icelandic waters, even less of a picnic then than now. Herring fishing kept the town going for centuries, but it had to endure many long spells of poverty. From 1939 onwards it bore the brunt of repeated, savage attacks by the Luftwaffe. It lives off the sea but has always had to fight the sea. Its lifeboat station was founded in 1801, 23 years before the Royal National Lifeboat Institution came into being. In 1807 the *Frances Ann*, the first lifeboat to be equipped with sails, was launched, and in her 48 years of gruelling service saved over 300 lives. A memorial to other men of this mettle in the Royal Naval Patrol Service stands in Belle Vue Park, carrying a saddeningly long roll-call of officers and men who 'have no grave but the sea'.

Immediately behind the entrance gates of the same park is a crumpled hummock of stones and cement which once formed the foundation of an early beacon, its purpose now better served by the lighthouse some 20 or 30 yards away. Wood for the light had to be humped up iron steps to maintain the fire, which must have consumed huge quantities of fuel and human effort.

A bygone rector was asked to go aboard a ship lying in the harbour early one morning to carry out a brief service over a dying seaman. The deceased was then buried quickly in Lowestoft churchyard so that the ship could set sail again without delay. The contents of the grave were not allowed to rest for long: that same day it was dug up, to yield not a corpse but a profitable consignment of lace.

Hewling Luson, lord of the manor of Gunton, owed much of his prosperity to his fleet of fishing luggers. When he married and brought his wife home from London, he was 'met at Mutford Bridge by near 400 horsemen and 40 coaches and chaises'. In 1756 he discovered an extensive clay formation at Corton Denes on his estate, and opened a porcelain factory. He had trouble with his workmen and was supplanted by another factory which opened the following year. The techniques employed followed closely those of the Bow porcelain manufacturers, and some of the underglaze blue pieces common to both factories are difficult to tell apart. It was reported that an employee was infiltrated into Bow to steal trade secrets.

Views of the town were frequently used, and simple blue Chinese landscapes in panels on a powder-blue ground proved very popular. A family working here gave its name to the Redgrave blue and red design. One distinctive product was a birth tablet on which could be lettered a child's name and birth date. Very few figurines were ever made. In 1803 the factory closed. Norwich Castle holds a good range of characteristic specimens, and the transfers used for decorating the china are preserved in Yarmouth Public Library.

Denmark Road recalls not the invaders of the distant past but friendlier relationships of the 1850s, when a brisk trade in cattle was carried on by the North Europe Steam Navigation Company between Lowestoft and Denmark. The landing of beasts at the old market often proved uproarious, especially when some escaped, as they frequently did, and ran amok through the streets.

The creation of an effective inner harbour by cutting the present channel from the outer harbour through to Lake Lothing caused a great deal of trouble in its early stages. Jealous Yarmouth authorities, merchants and shipowners made concerted attempts to thwart the development of Lowestoft's facilities. Work was nevertheless completed, and then there were further ambitious plans for opening up a navigable waterway as far as Norwich. This proved impracticable, and Lowestoft's growth was halted for a time until Morton Peto put forward his scheme for laying a railway to Reedham to connect with the Norwich line.

It was in the year of *The Romany Rye* that Borrow met Edward FitzGerald, who spent some time in Lowestoft and used to wander about the shore after dark, 'longing for some fellow to accost me who might give some promise of filling up a very vacant place in my heart'. His desire was eventually satisfied when he met Joseph Fletcher, a red-haired sailor known to everyone as Posh. FitzGerald grew sentimental about Posh as he had done about so many friends of his youth. At one stage he commissioned the building of a herring lugger, the *Meum and Teum*, which they would operate together, but in the end it was handed over to Posh to run as he chose.

Another sailor working in the fishing trade was Joseph Conrad, who first set foot on English soil here and was to refer to the town afterwards as his spiritual birthplace. He was for some time a deckhand on a Lowestoft trawler before committing himself to the equally hazardous life of a writer.

From words to music: Benjamin Britten, son of a Lowestoft dentist, was in America early in the war but became homesick when he read in *The Listener* an article by E. M. Forster about George Crabbe and his environment. Before the war he had bought and restored a mill at Snape, near Aldeburgh: it was to this, and not to Lowestoft, that he returned.

Lowestoft has spread, sprouting its own suburbs and making suburbs out of adjoining villages. Pakefield has become part of the coastal holiday strip. A few miles further south, Kessingland remains detached but has much the same ambience: holiday camp, caravans, and shingle. The Suffolk Wild Life Park beside the A.12 at the southern end of the village has roomy paddocks for small and large animals, and a large walk-in aviary where visitors can play the part of moving perches for a variety of parrots and macaws. There are also a picnic area, a children's playground, and a stream which may be fished on payment of a small fee.

Bombs dropped during Nazi raids severely damaged, among other homes, California House and Nugget Cottages. These were built by the great-grandfather of a present Kessingland resident on his return from the Klondyke with spoils which included a large gold nugget. He also invested in some fishing boats. The nugget was brought out on special occasions and shown to his children and grandchildren; for the rest of the year it was hidden away, and the family were assured that it would be disposed of only in dire emergency. The old man died without leaving any clue to its hiding-place. During repairs to the bomb damage a search was made for the golden heirloom, but no trace of it has ever been found. Possibly during the decline of his fishing venture its owner reached a moment of crisis which could reasonably be declared, if only to himself, a dire emergency.

Throughout several hundred years there are references to a ferry between Kessingland and Covehithe, where in 1308 one John de Cove had his hythe, or landing stage, for loading and unloading vessels. The ferry had its tragedies: in 1611 it was recorded that 'about 16 persons were drowned on the 26th July coming from the fair, by reason of a cable crossing the haven'.

Access to Covehithe today is down a long branch from the main road through Wrentham. The size of the church tower, one of the most imposing seamarks along these crumbling cliffs, promises a community of some importance; but there are only a few cottages below its impressive bulk. Of all the isolated churches in Suffolk apparently erected with no consideration for the existence or otherwise of a possible congregation, few can be as disproportionate as St Andrew's. It was probably built in the early fifteenth century by a rich incumbent, but can never have boasted any large attendance. By the seventeenth century it was already in a dangerous condition, and permission was given for parts of the structure to be pulled down and used in the construction of the present condensed church within the shell of the old. Walberswick, a little way south across the Blyth, has been treated in much the same way.

There are interesting walks along the edge of the low cliffs sloping down to the uncluttered shore by Benacre Broad with its fringe of copse, or towards Easton Bavents and Southwold. They are all the more interesting to regular visitors who can watch the retreat of the clifftop path, gnawed away and forced persistently back, establishing a new track which will itself soon be in peril.

The title page of Thomas Gardner's history, published in 1754, sums up as graphically as one could wish the shifting fortunes of the Suffolk coastline:

AN

HISTORICAL ACCOUNT

OF

DUNWICH,

Antiently a CITY, now a BOROUGH;

BLITHBURGH,

Formerly a TOWN of NOTE, now a VILLAGE,

SOUTHWOLD,

Once a VILLAGE, now a TOWN-CORPORATE

The Danes, the Dutch and the French have all in their time harassed communities down this strip of land, but none has ever done as much damage as the sea. To this day there is no coast road. It is not possible to say, 'Let's drive down through Southwold and Dunwich, and go on to Aldeburgh.' You must continually branch off and come back in, out and back in again. There is little more than a mile between Southwold and Walberswick across the marshes, but by road the journey is some eight miles round the river Blyth and its inland mudflats. Constant erosion has kept the trunk road builders at a safe distance.

The Blyth originally flowed into the sea near Dunwich, but in 1590 the channel which now cuts Southwold off from Walberswick was dug. As ships increased in size they found it difficult to reach Blythburgh, whose quays were now, in any case, proving inadequate. When a bad fire followed the decline in trade, most of the townspeople decided to move out and settle elsewhere. They left behind them their massive church, rearing up from the heath like an austere cathedral.

Monks from a neighbouring priory, a limb of St Osyth's Abbey in Essex, began the building of the church in 1412. Work continued for 80 years. In 1577 a great storm shattered the door during a service and brought the steeple down through the roof. Two members of the congregation were killed, and many others avowed that they had been burnt by the Devil himself. Scorch marks can still be seen on the north door.

The steeple was never replaced, and after the abandonment of the town the church decayed. During Cromwell's time the fanatical Dowsing brought men here to destroy all traces of idolatry, and hundreds of bullets were fired into the woodwork, including the angels in the roof. For some time the Roundheads used the church as a stable, and traces of their tethering rings can still be found in the pillars of the nave. A writer in 1819 describes the windows 'miserably patched up' with bricks and mortar, the interior carvings 'daubed with whitewash' and fragments from the roof, including angels' wings, reduced to 'a promiscuous heap of lumber' in a corner of the churchyard. As late as the 1870s, when the church was in partial use, there were reports of the congregation having to use umbrellas to protect themselves against rain pouring in through the roof.

In 1881 restoration began, and has continued slowly and doggedly ever since. The church now serves not only as a place of worship but as an inspiring setting for musical recitals, including some of the annual Aldeburgh Festival concerts. It was invaluable in 1969, when several major programmes had to be transferred at short notice from the burnt-out Maltings at Snape. If the listener's attention strays during a concert he can always entertain his eyes with a study of the inventive, often irreverent bench ends, including a fine septet of Deadly Sins: Avarice, Hypocrisy, Pride, Gluttony (bulging painfully as the result of excesses); Drunkenness, Sloth, and Slander (a tell-tale-tit with her split tongue hanging out).

Generous 'Friends of Blythburgh' have installed and pay for floodlighting of the church on many evenings of the year. It is an unforgettable sight, floating and glistening through the haze off the saltings, or bright and clear against a deep blue sky.

From below the church there are long walks across the open tracts of Wenhaston Common, or seawards along footpaths through the Heronry and on to Walberswick.

In the reign of Henry VIII the mainstays of the Icelandic fishing trade, along with Lowestoft, were Southwold, Covehithe, Walberswick and Dunwich. Some venturers died in northern waters, some settled in Iceland and never returned. To balance this, many Icelanders worked on the returning boats and settled here. Their

influence and that of other Scandinavians is preserved in many sur-
names and place names, and in the countenance of many a man
and woman.

The Danish author Knud Sønderby wrote: 'One feels that one can
get the whole of Denmark in the hollow of one's hand, relive one's
own life simply by remembering harbours.' The same might well be
said of this fissured, unstable coastline, but perhaps the word 'remembering' is even more appropriate here, since changes wrought
by the ravenous North Sea have often been so devastating that
many great harbours and ports have left nothing but a memory.

On Southwold beach today, a wind blowing from the north-east
will urge the water to bring a fine carpet of sand from the Yarmouth banks. A shift of wind, and the sand is dragged out again, leaving escarpments of pebbles. The tide is said to be 'making' or
'scouring'. In the long term there has been more assiduous scouring
than making along these shores.

In Defoe's day, Southwold—or, as it was then known, Swole or
Southole—had but one industry, the curing of sprats 'in the same
manner as they do herrings at Yarmouth, that is to say, speaking in
their own language, they make red sprats, or to speak good English,
they make sprats red'. When Defoe was writing thus, Southwold
and Dunwich were in one of their periods of depression, and Walberswick was getting the best of the trade. To seamen from farther
north there was little to choose between them:

> *Swoul and Dunwich and Walderswick*
> *All go in at one lousy creek.*

Defoe also wrote, some 50 years after the event, about the battle
of Sole Bay between the Dutch and English fleets. Modern accounts
refer to a Dutch defeat at the hands of the English, but Defoe was
of the opinion that the English were in fact worsted, and Pepys's own
account would seem to confirm this.

In 1672 the Dutch were preparing a massive assault on England.
They tried to repeat their earlier Medway triumph by attacking up
the Thames, but although they succeeded in blockading London for

a brief period they were forced to withdraw. James, Duke of York, High Admiral of the Fleet, made Southwold his headquarters in company with his cousin Prince Rupert and the Earl of Sandwich, and the French and English fleets anchored in uneasy alliance along a line between Easton Bavents and Minsmere to await news of the next Dutch foray, which was sure to come soon.

The Dutch did not delay. They moved so fast that they were within two hours' sailing of the allied fleets before their presence was even noticed. The French swiftly detached themselves and, as treacherous as most Englishmen had feared, headed south and kept out of harm's way. Men carousing ashore in the Southwold hostelries, doubtless as enjoyable then as they are now, were hastily rounded up and sent out to do battle. The Duke of York's ships met the full fury of De Ruyter's magnificently gunned fleet. The Earl of Sandwich went down with his ship when it was exploded by a Dutch fireship, and his corpse washed up by the tide some days later could be identified only by the star he wore on his charred uniform and by three rings in his pocket. The Duke of York had to abandon first one flagship and then another.

The slaughter was terrible. De Ruyter himself was injured, and the attackers were glad at last to sail back to Holland. Both sides claimed the victory. It was in fact somewhat of a stalemate. England had not smashed the Dutch fleet, which remained in command of the seas; but the Dutch had been forced to withdraw without inflicting the irreparable defeat which was essential to their war aims.

Southwold today has a population of about 2,000. It gives the appearance of being a decorous little retreat for the aged, with just enough old-fashioned, courteous shopkeepers to supply their needs, and just enough children to grow into adolescence as shop assistants. Some residents would like to preserve it in just such an equilibrium; but there is far more to the town than that. Younger people who have once visited it come back again and again, heedless of the fact that its pre-war pier has been sliced down to a stump and that there are no cinemas and no other 'entertainments'. They marvel at themselves; but summer after summer they come back. It is, if anything, even more delightful in winter, with a quiet chuckling, busy little life of its own. Like the people, its side streets, lanes and quiet corners are both self-deprecating and self-assured. Its wobbly promenade, its perky, brightly painted beach huts and even its Victorian seafront terraces all have that undefinable something: they have style. Those of us who live here....

Yes, I confess I have left it a bit late to declare my interest. I live in Southwold and can imagine living nowhere else. In winter our windows are so encrusted with salt that it is hard to see out. A gale plays tunes through our teeth; and the most that any local will say is, 'It's airy'. But the sun over the rim of the world greets us before anyone else; and the evening skies, each evening new and unrepeatable, strike sparks from the church tower, the river below the Common, and the lighthouse behind us. The authorities who built that lighthouse in 1899 were taking no chances: knowing the unreliability of the cliff edge, they set it well back behind the first row of houses.

The open greens introduced after the fire of 1659 have given Southwold a shape which no rebuilding or piecemeal restyling can alter, unless some future borough council or county authority sells our inheritance for some further North Sea gas development or for conversion into a profitable holiday camp, which we like to think is improbable. From South Green it is possible to take in sea, marsh and the spread of Regency houses, converted cottages, and the radiant little gardens of Constitution Hill all in one slow, appreciative rotation. But each green has its own charm: East Green with its composition of inn, painted doors and lighthouse; Bartholomew Green with the Dutch-gabled museum in one direction, the whole length of the church in the other; and St James' Green with its nautical flavour of mast, flagpoles and smartly repainted ships' figureheads.

St Edmund's church is not generally regarded as highly as Lavenham or Long Melford, but its overall coherence makes up for any shortcomings in detail. Flushwork is restricted to panels on and between buttresses, and the chequered walls of the south porch. Also around the porch is a sequence of the Virgin Mary's initial M. Its upper room served first as the priest's chamber and then as an ammunition store, a school, and a tiny museum.

One of the glories of the sea-bright interior is the painted screen, including the 12 apostles with St Paul curiously replacing St Matthias. The carvings on the choir stalls are admirably frivolous. There is a Seven Sacraments font, common in East Anglia but rare elsewhere. This example was disfigured by Dowsing, who at the same time destroyed the cover; a modern replacement was provided in 1935.

Overlooking the font is a 'Jack-o'-the-Clock', whose striking of the bell to announce the beginning of service was once operated from a clock mechanism: today he is set in motion by a tug on the rope. The armour he wears is that of the Wars of the Roses, and since a white rose emblem is carved on the south porch and on the north doors of the church it would appear that he was a Yorkist.

A new 'Southwold Jack' appeared in 1969, faithfully modelled in fibreglass and set upon the office block of Adnams' brewery, one of the last independent brewers in Eastern England and one of the finest, which has for generations used the figure as its trademark. In 1970 they took a step applauded by all traditionalists: they reintroduced horse-drawn drays for deliveries within five or six miles of Southwold.

Southwold Jack has survived. Adnams' have survived. In spite of bombing and the loss of all its Victorian stained glass (perhaps no great loss, that), the church has survived. The guns presented to the town by 'Butcher' Cumberland have survived and still stand on Gun Hill. The Southwold Railway has unfortunately not survived.

A private company was responsible for the operation of this railway, founded in 1879 and working for half a century. A narrow gauge line carried passengers, luggage and coal from Halesworth to Southwold and carried passengers, luggage, fish and milk churns in the opposite direction. The difference in gauge between this and the main line meant that everything had to be unloaded at Halesworth and re-loaded into the normal Great Eastern trucks.

Wenhaston was the only intermediate station for the first few years, then Blythburgh and Walberswick were added. Between Walberswick and Southwold a swing bridge was erected to cross the river Blyth, and to avoid any danger of this being inadvertently open for boats while a train was approaching, the key of the bridge had to be handed to the driver at Southwold and left with the Blythburgh stationmaster for collection on the return journey.

Although the spread of car and bus traffic finally put the railway out of business in 1929, the path of the old line can still be easily traced, and makes an agreeable walk from Southwold to Walberswick, crossing the river by a bailey bridge. To drive between the two places it is necessary to go inland to the A.12, branch off at Blythburgh, and turn yet again at the B.1387 across land which often appears to be on fire: broom flickers yellow against heath and trees, echoed on approaching the village by forsythia in expansive gardens; and in the bareness of winter the grass and bracken are as brown as scorched toast. Walberswick has a much sandier shore than most hereabouts, backed by shifting dunes which have failed to hold back the sea on several recent occasions. Its holiday houses, shacks and huts keep respectfully apart from the prim, pretty residential village. There are footpaths across the marshes and through the woods to Dunwich. Driving to Dunwich, one resumes the in-out game, returning to the B.1125 and then swinging back down the first left turn. Some little way down this road the Forestry Commission have provided a picnic place.

Dunwich today is a cluster of small houses, a pub, a tiny barn of a museum, and the husk of a friary which shelters farm machinery and some fidgety hens. There are a few fishing boats, a rusty winch, and a line of tank-trap blocks. Yet in the days of Sigebert and Egric, this town had precedence over all others in the kingdom of East Anglia. It continued to flourish. In 1208 King John granted a charter for which Dunwich had to pay a fee of 200 marks, 10 falcons, and 5 gerfalcons. For rights over all wrecks on its shore it had to pay the Crown, in addition, 5,000 eels annually.

This would have been no great imposition. The eel population thrives in the marshes to this day, and eel pritching is an old-established method of capture. In the mud of ditch bottoms one looks for two small holes. These are the eel's blow-holes, and between them lies the eel. The pritch, a spear with four or five sharp hooks turned inwards, is jabbed forcefully and repeatedly down into the mud until an eel is trapped within the hooks and lifted dripping from the slime, lashing in a frenzy. Anyone who has been out on an expedition of this kind will remember it in his wrists and shoulders for the next 24 hours.

A body of the King's Galleys was stationed at Dunwich—five galleys, as in London, while Ipswich had only two. In 1242, when Henry III's truce with the French was broken, Dunwich was ordered to provide aid by sea and land. Still the major Suffolk port, it owned some 80 ships. It had a daily market, and important annual fairs. There were seven known churches and many chapels.

In 1328 a great storm choked the harbour. A new harbour was built, then a third and a fourth; but the sea was remorseless, and by 1540 less than a quarter of the old city remained. Gradually the land was scraped away until the water reached the edge of the market-place. In 1739 came the final onslaught. A gale smashed into the cliffs and dragged down nearly all that was left of Dunwich.

Still the name retained its proud privileges. Two members of Parliament were returned for this 'rotten borough' until 1820.

The church of All Saints clung to the edge of the cliff for many decades, but in 1921 its precarious tower finally succumbed, and now its only traces are a few chunks of masonry along the shore below.

Old fishermen claim that when they were young it was still possible to hear the bells of drowned churches jangling in the current, and that the phosphorescence of bones in the old graveyards can even now be seen shining from the cliff face at night. Old fishermen, however, are all too sociably eager to tell their audience what it shiveringly wishes to hear.

The sailors and traders are gone and forgotten, but one of Dunwich's sons has the right to lasting fame. John Daye was born here in 1522, destined to become the first printer to cut and use Anglo-Saxon type in England and to produce one of the earliest almanacs and the famous *Foxe's Book of Martyrs*. He is buried on the far side of the county in Little Bradley, where a splendidly poetic brass commemorates the man, his work, and his family. He had two wives, of whom it is written: EACH WYFE TWELVE BABES AND EACH

33 *Ipswich: Christchurch Mansion (sixteenth and seventeenth centuries)*

OF THEM ONE MORE ... an appropriate number of offspring for a man who made such noble use of those other 26 characters.

Above the village rises Dunwich Common, taken over by the National Trust in 1968. Its heathery plateau commands wide views over marsh, forest and sea. To the south the hulk of Sizewell atomic power station rises from the rippling land like the conning-tower of some monstrous apocalyptic submarine. It is especially sinister when seen through a haze of rain or mist, but in a matter of seconds the haze may clear, the vast sky will be filled with toppling clouds, and the power station will be as sharp-edged as the jet racing across the sky to the U.S.A.F. base near Woodbridge, or the tanker and timber-boat tight-roping along the seaward edge of the world.

Between the Common and Sizewell lies Minsmere, once the home of the first Leiston Abbey, which was moved in 1363 from the dank marsh to the higher ground where its ruins now stand. Today Minsmere is a nature reserve, a tawny expanse of reeds which blur and change texture under every stroking movement of wind and light. The reeds crowd closer to the sea than one might expect. Their phalanxes bolster up the marram grass in its task of trapping wind-blown sand, and they stand up to incursions of salt water because the peat and clay in which they are rooted absorbs enough rain water to keep them supplied. Two observation hides within reach of the shore path may be visited if permits have previously been obtained from the warden.

In spite of its four-square aggressiveness in this landscape, the power station is not as ugly as many of its kind. A conifer plantation softens its starkness, a bright grassy slope leads gently down towards the sand dunes, and there are sorties of gorse right into the dunes. The nearby inn is called, aptly enough, the 'Vulcan Arms'. It was in fact called this long before the atomic generators came—probably associated, like the 'Engineers' Arms' in nearby Leiston, with the engineering works there.

The firm of Richard Garrett were early specialists in agricultural machinery, much of it exported to Russia and South America. Traction engines and other equipment from the factory still show up at veteran car and steam engine rallies, and a fair amount of its ironwork can be seen in grave surrounds or decorations in local church-yards. In 1859 a branch line of the East Suffolk Railway came in here to cope with increasingly heavy transport needs, lasting almost a century before being demolished at Beeching's behest. The town's industry has kept it in healthy condition ever since, and plans to increase the output at Sizewell should help the local employment situation.

Leiston is perhaps best known to the outside world as the home of Summerhill, A. S. Neill's provocatively experimental school.

I have spoken blithely of the view of Sizewell from Dunwich as though it were simple to reach one from the other. On foot it is not too complicated. By car, one must zig-zag again. The road from Dunwich to Leiston and onwards passes through Theberton, the birthplace of C. M. Doughty, whose *Travels in Arabia Deserta* took him far from these Anglian pastures. In the churchyard a rusty machine-gun marks the grave of 16 men from a Zeppelin brought down in June 1917. A story is told that the reason for the dirigible's dropping of a bomb and thus for its subsequent crash was that the crew heard the jingle of harness from army horses in a field below. If there is any truth in the tale, which I doubt, the Zeppelin engines must have been less deafening than modern jets.

Leiston Abbey ruins beside the road are those of the Premon-stratensian foundation which was resettled here after abandoning Minsmere. Its new home was burnt down in 1389 but rebuilt on this same site. The restored Lady Chapel now serves as a diocesan retreat.

There are two ways into Aldeburgh from Leiston, one over the heath, flanked by expensive modern houses, and the other turning left at Aldringham crossroads to reach Thorpeness between some ancient tumuli and across a golf course. A windmill marks the out-skirts of this peculiar coastal settlement, and beside it is a disguised water-tower known as the 'House in the Clouds' which does in fact contain living quarters. The brick fantasy on our left looks old-world at first glance . . . olde-worlde at second glance . . . incredible on further contemplation. The village is not just a 'folly' but a collection of follies. Much of it is half-timbered in a style which can only be classified as Stockbroker's Clerk's Tudor.

It is all the brainchild of G. Stuart Ogilvie, who bent his endeavours just before and after the First World War to the conversion of the original fishing village and its ramshackle huts into 'a corner of Merrie England' complete with Assembly Rooms and a Sports Club. The waters of the Meare were opened to the public, and its little islets were bedecked as 'The Pirates' Lair', 'Treasure Island', and so on.

The utter absurdity of Thorpeness is not merely harmless but enjoyable. A writer who rented a house there some winters ago in search of peace and quiet describes the experience as being 'like living on an abandoned film set'. In summer it is brighter, busier, amusing, agreeable. Rowing a skiff round the shallow mere (Meare, locally) is safe for children and offers the adult more scope than the usual cramped boating lake.

If desperation creeps in, there is always the swift route along the hedgeless and fenceless road to Aldeburgh, parallel with the sea on one hand and, on the other, the old railway track half a mile inland.

A year after it reached Leiston, the line was extended to Aldeburgh. Wilkie Collins must have been an early passenger: his novel, *No Name*, contains a chapter set in 'Aldborough' and describes in detail Crag Path, named after the Coralline and Red Crags which, formed here by warm seas in prehistoric times, have crumbled before the assault of colder seas in more recent centuries. Today, under tarmac, Crag Path is Aldeburgh's equivalent of a promenade, flanked on one side by a row of ugly, irregular, individually entertaining houses and converted cottages, and on the other by a wall retaining the shingle.

There is very little that is truly old in the present 'Old Castle' from which its name derives. The Moot Hall which once stood well inland and is now close to the seafront is the nearest thing to an authentic survival, and even so has been greatly changed: a sixteenth-century building which originally had an open area at ground floor level, it has been restored and enclosed to form a council chamber and a museum of old maps and prints. A Martello tower, one of that chain stretching down through Kent and Sussex, was built at about the time when other contractors were trying to make Aldeburgh a watering place fit to compete with the south coast.

One of the Victorian developers was Newson Garrett, who also built the extensive Maltings at Snape. His daughter Elizabeth and her family are buried in the churchyard. Elizabeth Garrett Anderson was the first woman doctor in England, and in 1908 became England's first lady Mayor.

The church is built largely of flint and not, as might have been expected, of the local Crag. It has been the scene of ship auctions, performances by Elizabethan strolling players, and, in our own time, concerts and recitals, some of them contributing to the cost of repairing the tower. In the days of the freebooting 'Dunkirkers' from the Netherlands there was a lantern-house on the tower, where a beacon was lit to raise the alarm.

Also interred here, in 1831, was Leveson Verney, a man now forgotten as possibly he would himself have wished to be forgotten. He grew up with the conviction that the less he saw of daylight the longer he would live, so he avoided the major temptations and perils of existence by sleeping all day and going out to visit his friends at night. I suspect that Verney found his friends diminishing in number as time went on, or at the very least growing irascible and less welcoming. When he died he left instructions that he was to be buried after dark without fuss. Such is the perversity of human nature that news of his surreptitious funeral circulated rapidly, and the streets were as full of torches and jollification as many a Suffolk street is on Bonfire Night.

'There is no sea like the Aldeburgh sea', said FitzGerald. 'It talks to me.' It has talked to many people in many voices, often too aggressively. The original town which won its wealth from trading, shipbuilding and fishing hardly exists today. The sea from which the inhabitants wrested that wealth came to reclaim it. Slaughden, once the port and business centre, is now only a name. A modern yacht club building stands on a narrow spit of land between the sea and the river Alde, writhing on its way to join the Ore behind Orford Ness, past forbidden wastes where research on secret weapons is carried out, and past Havergate Island, also banned to unauthorized visitors but hospitable towards the avocet and other rare birds.

George Crabbe worked for a time in a warehouse on Slaughden Quay and detested it. Perhaps it was as an antidote to these unwelcome labours that he was impelled to begin writing. His earliest poems are naïve, and indeed there was always to be a dogged clumsiness in his work which prevented his reaching the highest peaks. But it is this bluntness, this earthiness of his—'a Pope in worsted stockings'—which gives his verse its own special power. He was brought up in full awareness of the cruelty of the elements and the cruelty of man to man. His report of the terrifying inundations of 1779 is still vivid: we feel ourselves with him in the family cottage, the water three feet deep in their ground-floor room, and we get a wry indication of family priorities when his father carries the cask of gin upstairs while his mother rescues the kettle.

George Crabbe was born on Christmas Eve, 1754, in a house which long ago surrendered to the waves. His grandfather was Collector of Customs but must have died in straitened circumstances since George's father, originally destined for trade, was reduced to keeping a parochial school in the porch of Orford church. For a while he went to live in a village near Loddon, in Norfolk, but duly returned to Aldeburgh and, after acting for some years as warehouse keeper and deputy collector, became collector of salt duties. He married a publican's widow and they had six children, of whom George was the eldest.

The boy showed little aptitude for the local trade of fishing. He went to school in Bungay and then, when it was suggested he might become a doctor, to a school kept by Richard Haddon of Stowmarket. After leaving school there was the unwelcome spell of servitude on the quay, until at last he was apprenticed to a Woodbridge surgeon and, at the age of 18, fell in love with Sarah Elmy of Parham.

Sarah was too shrewd to become the wife and drudge of a young man with so few prospects. No happier in his medical work than he had been with warehouse chores, Crabbe did what many a young man has done before and since: he went to London to seek fame and fortune, believing that he had it in him to become a successful poet. He addressed himself to various noble lords and hoped-for patrons, at first in resounding verse but all too soon in begging letters. At times he was in danger of being imprisoned for debt. It was not until Edmund Burke took him under his wing that his fortunes changed for the better. Even then, he stood little chance of producing the equivalent of a modern best-seller. It was on Burke's advice, following a lengthy discussion about his real vocation, that he took examinations for holy orders and was ultimately ordained by the Bishop of Norwich. He returned to Aldeburgh as a curate, and lost no time in hurrying to Parham to see his beloved again.

She was still not prepared to risk marrying him. Burke, again pulling strings, won him the appointment of chaplain to the Duke of Rutland, so once again George Crabbe left his home town. Yet at the same time it could be said that he carried it with him wherever he went. All the things he burned to say had been kindled in Aldeburgh. The hates and pettinesses of Aldeburgh were, and always would be, of greater significance than any pleasures he might experience elsewhere.

It was while in the Duke's service that, in 1783, he published his long poem *The Village*, and suddenly became a literary lion.

When the Duke was sent to Ireland as Lord Lieutenant, Crabbe sought leave to remain in England. He could not bear to be so far away from his adored Miss Elmy. Granted two livings in Dorset, he at last found himself in a position to plead his suit convincingly; and at last was accepted. They were married at Beccles.

He was none too conscientious about his Dorset parishes, preferring the east of England, and did not scruple to use his influential friends to get his own way. Gradually he edged back, via livings in Leicestershire and Lincolnshire. Whenever possible he and his wife visited Parham, until the day when the family house which had happy memories for both of them became Sarah's, after some less happy but all too common squabbling among relations. The present Parham Hall stands on the site of this house, not to be confused with the beautiful moated brick farmhouse now known as Moat Hall.

Closer than ever to home, Crabbe became curate of Swefling and nearby Glemham. He continued writing and even ventured on three novels, all of which he destroyed; and having almost completed a treatise on botany in English, he was persuaded to destroy this, too, on the grounds that it was monstrously vulgar, in every sense of the word, to write such a work in any tongue other than Latin. He returned to the practice of verse and in 1810 finished a work into which he had put his heart and soul. His son records that 'Mr Hatchard put it to the press: it was published in 1810, and in 1816 it had attained its sixth edition'. It was *The Borough*.

This provided a vivid and by no means flattering picture of Aldeburgh. Hazlitt wrote that it was 'done so to the life, that it seems almost like some sea-monster, crawled out of the neighbouring slime, and harbouring a breed of strange vermin, with a strong local scent of tar and bilge-water'. He was happy neither about the style nor the author's motives: 'The situation of a country clergyman is not necessarily favourable to the cultivation of the Muse. He is set down, perhaps, as he thinks, in a small curacy for life, and he takes his revenge by imprisoning the reader's imagination in luckless verse.'

The poem was to provide the basis for another work of a kind which might well have baffled Crabbe, who had no ear whatsoever for music. As Crabbe had yearned for his home county when only a few hundred miles away, so Benjamin Britten in America felt the undertow of the Aldeburgh tides. He found himself committed to the composition of *Peter Grimes*, whose first performance marked the reopening of Sadler's Wells after the war and also the first real international breakthrough by an English operatic composer.

Since 1948 there has been an annual Aldeburgh Festival of Music and the Arts. Some lines from *The Borough* seem apposite today:

> *Soon as the season comes, and crowds arrive,*
> *To their superior rooms the wealthy drive.*
> *Others look round for lodging snug and small,*
> *The brick-floored parlour which the butcher lets ...*

I confess that I have not verified whether or not the present butchers have brick-floored parlours, or whether they let them to holidaymakers.

Even the non-musical feel the pulse in the air during June. Certain other pulses are blessedly missing for a while, or at any rate more distant. The official programme booklet dutifully thanks the U.S.A.F. for revising its flying schedules in order not to conflict with concerts. When a staggering thunderstorm once shook Blythburgh church during an austerely religious Schutz programme, forcing on Peter Pears and others a few bars' rest not shown in the score, I overheard the observation: 'The Almighty isn't as considerate as the United States Air Force.'

The Festival has by now spread itself over the surrounding countryside. Concerts, recitals, operas and cantatas have been given in churches in Framlingham, Orford, Wenhaston and Southwold. There are 'church crawls' and nature walks, lectures, exhibitions. The church and Jubilee Hall in Aldeburgh are still used, but the heart of all this activity is really no longer in Aldeburgh but at Snape.

The A.1094 leads straight out of town beside the golf course for about four miles before reaching the crossroads by Snape church. A left turn takes one down into the little village and on to the wharf beside which stand the Maltings. The windmill above the farm on the far side of the road is that in which Britten and Peter Pears live and work.

Conversion of the malt-house into a concert hall was made possible by grants from the Arts Council, the Gulbenkian Foundation, and the Decca record company, plus some £80,000 offered in private donations. The hall was opened by the Queen in 1967, and its conversion was included in the annual Civic Trust awards for distinguished new buildings and schemes. It has been used in season and out of season. Splendid recordings have been made here. The acoustics are incomparable. In this unlikely spot by the Alde, by the inoffensive and undistinguished bridge which replaced a much loved, humpbacked landmark in order to facilitate the movement of material for the atomic power station, music of every kind has been played, broadcast and televized. There was even, to the bewilderment of many of the visiting American musicians concerned, a successful series sponsored by the B.B.C. of 'Jazz at the Maltings'.

In the interval of one concert, strolling along the grassy bank and looking out to the shimmering edge of the saltings and the tree-hazed upthrust of Iken, my wife and I wondered if this were in danger of becoming another, fashionable Glyndebourne. But then my wife said: 'There's a big difference so far—have you noticed that all the people we've passed have been talking about the *music*?' A valid distinction, and one which we hope will remain.

On the opening night of the 1969 Aldeburgh Festival, the interior of the concert hall was burnt out. It seemed, and still seems, incredible that here, in the heart of a countryside whose transport links are feebler than they were in the nineteenth century, and with such a disaster on their hands, the organizers were able to keep the programme going with only one omission. The Bishop of St Edmundsbury and Ipswich at once offered the unrestricted use of Blythburgh and Orford churches, and some concerts were given as far afield as Ely. One correspondent said that he 'sensed in the audience a feeling of identification which went far beyond sympathy—a steely determination that the values for which the festival stands shall not, and will not, be lost.'

The determination was there. It was announced that the hall should be rebuilt in time for the opening of the following season. It must be done; and it was done. Again the Queen came to Snape, and on the gloriously sunny afternoon of Friday 5 June 1970 a programme of *Music for a Royal Occasion* reopened the Maltings.

Backstage facilities were extended during the reconstruction, and many other improvements and additions are planned. It is hoped to have in due course a music library, an art gallery, studios and workshops. Master classes will be organized for advanced music students. There is to be a Sunday opera club, functioning all year round. The Maltings ought eventually to become an all-embracing arts centre, in a setting it would be hard to match.

The riverside walk from the quay to Iken cliff offers no scenic melodrama but is one of the most satisfying anywhere along this coast. The water, the reeds, the popping and plopping and rustling and the birdsong below the river wall, the dark barricade of inland forest, the tremor of skyline and the dizzy chasm of the sky itself, all unite to offer eternity in a summer afternoon and strange exhilaration on even the bleakest winter's day.

There is disquiet below this beauty. Several times the river wall has been breached, and unless it can be strengthened there is a danger of the marsh and its wild life being flooded by salt water, upsetting the whole balance of flora and fauna. The Blythburgh formation of mudflats could be repeated here.

For the present, all the elements are stabilized around, and given proportion by, the church tower of St Botolph, who built an abbey here on a hill which knew the Romans and near which, legend has it, some great pre-Roman queen fought a battle whose significance is quite lost to us.

This church is one of my earliest memories of Suffolk. When I first saw it, the graveyard was overgrown, and jagged teeth of headstones were jutting and lurching out from a crumbling cliff. The wind moaned in the trees. It was the setting for some bloodcurdling weird tale. The wind moans still, or shrills and sings in the eternally restless trees, and the slopes of the estuary are clamorous with sea and marsh birds; but the graves have been tidied up and there is a neat little plantation on the bank below. Nor is the church as it was. Like the Maltings, it has been afflicted by a destructive fire. A few years ago, sparks from a bonfire in the churchyard ignited the thatched roof and gutted the nave. All that remained were the scorched shell and the tower above the water, and, when I was last there, a new note to add to the other songs and murmurs and whispers: the sound of plastic sheeting flapping and booming against the ruins.

With so many churches crumbling into decay for want of funds, I felt gloomily that this lovely, isolated one at Iken stood little chance of being rebuilt. Happily I was wrong. A Faculty has been granted for its restoration—a restoration as important to the local community and its many friends as that of the Maltings.

CHAPTER SEVEN

Ore and Deben and Orwell

Tunstall Forest fringes the heathlands and darkly fingers out in the direction of the ancient oaks of Staverton, twisted into grotesque shapes, some of them locked in a bitter struggle with encroaching holly trees and brambles. Staverton Forest belonged first to Butley priory and then for centuries to generation after generation of one family.

The fourteenth-century gatehouse is all that remains of the Augustinian priory founded in 1171 by Ranulph de Glanville. Its lecture in stone heraldry encompasses the arms of England and France, the three crowns of East Anglia, the Passion, and the Holy Roman Empire. Below are set the escutcheons of great East Anglian families and officials. Buried somewhere within the grounds is Michael de la Pole, the Earl of Suffolk whose body was brought home from Agincourt and reputedly encased in a silver coffin; but nobody now knows the exact site.

The dusky woods are sunny in spring with daffodils. There may be primroses in the neighbourhood, there may not: ruthless hedging and ditching campaigns all too often uproot the primrose patches, and it is impossible to predict what any season will bring.

Inland through Tunstall the road takes in Campsey Ashe, where there was once an Augustinian nunnery. A lonely railway station proclaims itself 'Wickham Market for Campsey Ashe', though it might more accurately be labelled 'Campsey Ashe for Wickham Market', since the little town is quite some distance from its railway. Wickham long ago lost its market to Woodbridge and is now only a diffident cluster of houses and shops apologetically compressing the A.12 into a tricky defile which can be widened for the benefit of rattling, reeking lorries only at the expense of some romantically subfusc houses, Georgian brick and dusty doorways, cramped but sprightly gardens, and iron balconies. The original market square is occupied by a car park and public lavatories, in spite of which and in spite of the rarely muted through traffic, it retains its charm and comes quietly, sociably to life in the evening with its cheerful fish-and-chip shop and the glow from the old 'White Hart' inn. The church has an octagonal tower and a spire visible for miles from any direction.

Travelling the main road in the Ipswich direction we come to Ufford, which is made up of Upper Street here and Lower Street down beside the Deben. Ufford takes its name from the Uffinga or Wuffinga dynasty of East Anglian kings, among them the Redwald who first toyed with Christianity and then allowed himself to be drawn back into paganism. The royal seat was somewhere in the Rendlesham area. A silver crown tentatively identified as Redwald's was dug up in 1687 but melted down before any proper study could be made of it.

Today the grounds of vanished Rendlesham House are guarded by two grotesque lodges. Coming upon the spiky coronet of the one just off the Eyke to Tunstall road is like being abruptly confronted by an outsize, three-dimensional, pre-war toothpaste advertisement.

Once off the A.12 we are back in a less frenetic world, unless we stray beside another airfield, this one Bentwaters. Better to turn away through the woods. On the seaward side of the forest palisade Orford, never conceivably a holiday resort yet an irresistible lure to anyone visiting this coast once or a hundred times, smugly waits to be discovered once again.

Orford is another claimant to the title of Edmund's last battle-ground. One theory has it that the Danes landed here and sacked the town, defeated Edmund, and pursued him towards Sutton.

The trading and fishing port grew in importance from the ninth century onwards. It built and equipped men-of-war. Later there were sheep all around it, and rich wool merchants did for the church what their fellows had so lavishly done elsewhere. Orford began to lose ground only when Aldeburgh came to life in the sixteenth century. There was an attempt in 1813 to reconstruct the harbour in accordance with modern needs, but it was never carried through.

The little square has for some years now been dominated not by the usual regional smell of smoked sprats and herring but by more aristocratic smoked fish. In a little establishment of scrubbed table-tops secured to barrels, locally smoked salmon and trout may be eaten or bought to take away, together with smoked eel and even smoked chicken, and oysters from local beds. The road past the old 'Jolly Sailor' leads to a quay seething with boats, including a podgily undecorative ferry. You may sail up the Alde or down the Ore to the narrow opening between the mainland and the spit; but you may not cross to the Ness and its football-jersey lighthouse unless equipped with an official pass. The best view you are likely to get of it, and of Havergate Island, is from the top of the castle keep.

The three-storeyed keep is all that remains of the fortress built by Henry II to guard the harbour against invaders and the land against fretful barons. A local clayey limestone, septaria, much used over the centuries for its cementing qualities, played a large part in the construction. It became the home of the de la Poles and the Wing-fields, and in more recent times belonged to Sir William Wallace. It is now administered as an Ancient Monument, has been used as a suitably eerie setting for television thrillers, and performs a more practical duty as a daylight mark for mariners off the treacherous inshore banks, complementing the sweep of the lighthouse every five seconds throughout the hours of darkness.

The Ness has for decades been the home of secrets. Here Robert Watson-Watt, later Sir Robert, carried out his early experimental work on radar. In spite of frustrations and hideous failures just at times when it was most important to impress the top brass, he and his colleagues had an invigorating time here. In his autobiography he writes nostalgically of the delights of the windswept tongue of land and of the hospitality of the 'Crown and Castle' in Orford, a stone's throw from the lowering castle itself. The guests' lounge of the hotel was turned into a conference room where arguments crackled throughout the evening, sometimes hopeful, sometimes weary and pessimistic. Each morning the team left Orford quay, as workers today still leave, for the peninsula where work had to be continued no matter what the setbacks. Sir Robert, engagingly admitting a good conceit of himself, quotes the Duke of Wellington: 'By God! I do not think it would have been done if I had not been there!' He also does not think, or cannot be sure, that the beer at the 'Jolly Sailor' could have been the nectar and ambrosia he and his colleagues seemed afterwards to remember. On this point his memory did not betray him: the beer from Southwold remains ambrosial.

Radar research was later transferred to Bawdsey Manor, a little way down the coast, where in 1936 the first coastal warning station was successfully installed.

During the war there was further military activity in the region, when expanses of Shingle Street were used for target practice.

The groups of healthy and usually cheerful young men so frequently to be seen walking, running or indulging in other strenuous activities along the roads and paths here come from the open Borstal at Hollesley. An interesting contrast—the educational freedom of A. S. Neill's Summerhill versus the discipline of Hollesley or the boys' naval training establishment H.M.S. *Ganges* we shall later come to at Shotley!

The shifting bar and wayward currents make sailing in and out of the Deben a skilled and hazardous business. There was once a chain ferry for vehicles between Bawdsey and Felixstowe Ferry, but now there is only a rowing-boat for passengers. Upstream the river is gentler, and both sides of the elysian valley are best seen from the water. Ramsholt also had a ferry in times past, but now provides only a convivial anchorage for yachts, dinghies and cruisers. The church's round tower has a truly imposing setting.

Supporters of the view that Edmund was killed near the coast rather than at Hoxne favour an area east of Shottisham and Sutton, to which he would have fled from Orford or, according to others, from a final battle in Staverton Forest.

Sutton is inarguably associated with one royal death. Reached by a footpath from the junction of the B.1083 and a by-road from Hollesley stands a group of 11 barrows. They are protected by the Ministry of Public Building and Works, but are on private land and may be viewed only from the path. At the south-western end, near the wood, is the most famous of these mounds. Three barrows had already been excavated in 1938, revealing fragments of bone, bronze and pottery, and in one the decaying remains of a boat, when in 1939 this fourth tumulus revealed a loose ship nail and then other nails still in position. As the archaeologists carefully cleared away the earth with fingers and small tools—removing the spoil in the kitchen dustpan from Sutton Hoo—they unveiled, inch by inch, the 'ghost' of a clinker-built ship 90 feet long and 14 feet wide. Everything perishable had perished. The ship's timbers themselves could be traced only by the undisturbed pattern of iron clench-nails. A shaft through the mound was at first thought to have been a robber shaft, but this was later ruled out. Even if there had been any intruders, they had missed the real booty. In an unravaged burial chamber lay the treasure of an East Anglian king who died somewhere between A.D. 640 and 660. There was no sign of human remains. The funeral barrow may have been meant to serve as a cenotaph to a monarch buried, or perhaps drowned, elsewhere.

The Second World War broke out before the finds could be properly examined and evaluated. Hidden away from air raids, they were brought out again in 1945, and now their full splendour was revealed. There were an iron helmet girded with silver, a gilded shield and a sword with jewelled pommel and golden hilt, silver bowls and spoons, a purse still containing 40 gold coins, gold and jewelled clasps and buckles of exquisite workmanship, and a damaged musical instrument which was reconstructed as a quadrangular harp but has recently been shown to have been a round lyre. Cleaned and restored, these glorious relics are now on display in the British Museum

Whether we approach it by road or by water, Woodbridge is most inviting. It makes the best of both land and river. Starting as a Saxon settlement in the shallow valley, it eventually moved up the slope to form a larger community round what is now Market Hill. The name comes from a wooden bridge which once crossed one of the river's offshoots. A prosperous market town from earliest times, and also important in the great years of the wool industry, it added to its riches by installing quays along the Deben, shipping goods, building boats, and making ropes and sailcloth. In the fifteenth century a number of Flemish brewers settled here, as well as in Ipswich, and by the sixteenth century were actually exporting beer back to the Low Countries.

Boatbuilding continues to this day but almost exclusively for pleasure craft. There is a flourishing sailing club, and races and regattas play a large part in the social life of the town. Property prices rise as more and more people from Ipswich and London come in search of houses. Even if the railway line suffers closure, a swift drive into Ipswich still keeps London within tolerable commuting distance.

There are rewarding riverside walks, particularly that below Kyson Hill, which is National Trust property, to Kyson Point. The tide mill, now in process of restoration, was the last mill in the country to be tidally operated, and went on working until 1956. Every street in the town itself has its own joys: Dutch gables, Tudor brickwork and Georgian frontages not yet quite spoilt by too many gashes of modern shop windows. In New Street the 'Old Bell and Steelyard' has for its inn sign the ponderous device once used for weighing wagons and their loads of hay or corn. This was removed and taken to London for an exhibition at the end of the last century, and then reinstated in its present position.

Seckford Street and many other local features perpetuate the memory of Thomas Seckford, a prosperous sixteenth-century merchant. In 1570 he built the Shire Hall on Market Hill, originally supported on piers which allowed free passage for carts and other traffic through the open ground floor, used as a corn exchange. The enclosure of this, and the staircases and Dutch gables, came later. Seckford established almshouses on whose site there is now the bright nineteenth-century row of Seckford Hospital for the aged, and gave the town a school and a public dispensary. A survey of the whole county which he financed led to the publication of Christo-

35 *East Bergholt: St Mary the Virgin (1350-1550) with sixteenth-century bell-cage in foreground*

pher Saxton's Atlas. It has been hinted that his breadth of interests took in smuggling and that he was not above allowing his ships to dabble in a little piracy from time to time. The family home, Seckford Hall, stands a few miles away, near Great Bealings on the far side of the A.12 by-pass. It is now a well maintained hotel, preserving much of its original appearance and atmosphere.

Thomas Seckford is buried in St Mary's church, which has a richly patterned north porch and, within, a Seven Sacraments font. The Church Street entrance is graced by fine eighteenth-century wrought iron gates.

Woodbridge will always be associated with Edward FitzGerald, who lived for many years in rooms above a gunsmith's premises on Market Hill, now a hardware shop. There has been a great deal of controversy over the authenticity or otherwise of his translation of Omar Khayyam and even over the text from which he worked; but while the arguments, like our local tides, scour or make, FitzGerald's translation seems the one most likely to survive.

He was born in 1809 at Bredfield, the seventh child of first cousins, his mother being also the child of first cousins. She was a FitzGerald, her husband a Purcell: she was the one with the money and, we gather, the dominating character, and her husband made no demur over changing his name to suit her. The memorial tablets in Boulge church speak for themselves.

Young FitzGerald went to school in Bury St Edmunds. He proved to be an amiable, intelligent lad without any great ambition. He got on well with elderly eccentrics, of whom there was no lack in the neighbourhood. Squire Jenny lived in a house without carpets and kept his windows permanently open to admit visitors, rain and snow. Major Moor, another neighbour flattered by the boy's attentiveness, wore a white hat many sizes too large for him, collected images of Oriental gods, and loved to chat about his experiences in India and beyond. Edward's imagination was fired both by the exotic reminiscences and by the defiant eccentricities. Although he was to lead, on the whole, an introspective and secluded life, he was often flamboyant in his dress and utterances, and when one of his biographers refers to his innumerable friendships and his 'quiet

36-39   Follies: 36 Gatehouse, Rendlesham; 37 Gazebo, Long Melford Hall; 38 Temple, Euston Hall; 39 Freston Tower

benevolence' we have also to remember his spiteful jibe when he heard of the death of Elizabeth Barrett Browning, which brought down upon him Robert Browning's thunderous and justifiable wrath.

When he was 16 the family moved to Wherstead Lodge near Ipswich, and then 10 years later came back in the Woodbridge direction, to Boulge Hall. The hall itself was pulled down in 1956, leaving the extensive parkland without a real focus.

George Crabbe, son of the Aldeburgh poet, was appointed to the living of Bredfield and became another of FitzGerald's collection of lovable oddities. Crabbe had a disconcerting habit of praying aloud for any individual among his flock whom he felt needed special consideration—'including Mary Ann Cuthbert', he would intone, selecting the poor girl because of her dubious reputation in the district, and giving the rest of his congregation something to gossip about on their way home from service.

Young FitzGerald had enough money to live on and felt no great inclination to take up any especially arduous profession. He was a dilettante, enjoying many things but concentrating on few, preferring the company and conversation of friends, some of whom he was prone to idealize. When he moved into the two-roomed cottage at the gates of Boulge Park it was so that he might establish his own tempo of life. When he chose to be undisturbed, he remained indoors and wandered about unshaven between mounds of books, helping himself to a glass of beer when he felt like it from a barrel in one corner. If in sociable mood, he would walk miles to visit friends, and then return contentedly to his untidy hermitage.

In 1846 he met the son of an Ipswich corn merchant, a young man who later became Professor of Sanskrit at Cambridge and was the first to mention Omar Khayyam's name to FitzGerald. Interest kindled slowly, as with all FitzGerald's ventures. He dabbled, became more engrossed ... but was in no hurry.

Approaching 50, FitzGerald married, much against the advice of his friends and against his own real convictions. Lucy Barton was the daughter of an old Quaker friend from Boulge who had also been a friend of Charles Lamb. Bernard Barton worked as a bank clerk but longed to win critical acclaim and make a living from his verse.

Some years after he died and was buried in Woodbridge Quaker cemetery, his still devoted FitzGerald, as a labour of love, edited and wrote an introduction to an edition of these poems. In the same affectionate mood he had promised the father to look after Lucy, and in fact contributed a fair amount of financial help whenever she needed it. Any novelist could have foretold the inherent dangers of such a situation, the inevitable drift of events. They married in 1856; and at once he regretted it. The demure girl with whom he had been on warily friendly, somewhat avuncular terms all these years was now a wife, pleasant and dutiful, but considering it her right to be taken to parties and accompanied everywhere on visits and expeditions of her own choosing. A man of leisure, he could not escape by pleading that he must go to the office or spend some time away on a business trip. She tried to make him conform; shudderingly he evaded such commitments. Within a few months they had separated. FitzGerald was invariably courteous when writing to her or about her, but did not wish ever to meet her again: 'Every year and every day I am creeping out of the world in my own way.'

Seeking consolation in the bland stoicism of Omar Khayyam, he now immersed himself utterly in the translation of the *Rubáiyát*. On completion it languished in the offices of a magazine for a year, and was finally published in 1859 at FitzGerald's own expense. He sent copies to his friends and disposed of the rest to a bookseller who, unable to get rid of them at the price of one shilling each, sold them off at a penny each, when they were discovered by Rossetti and Swinburne.

It was in 1860 that Fitzgerald moved into Woodbridge, there to fill his rooms with the usual heaps of books. He had a small yacht built, and named it *The Scandal*, asserting that this was, after all, Woodbridge's main commodity. Many of his old friends had died, and though he made new ones among the Deben sailing fraternity, his pleasures were tinged with a nostalgia which throbbed through all he said and wrote.

My chief Amusement in Life is Boating, on River and Sea. The Country about here is the Cemetery of so many of my oldest

179

Friends: and the petty race of Squires who have succeeded only use the Earth for an *Investment*: cut down every old Tree: level every Violet Bank: and make the old Country of my Youth hideous to me in my Decline. There are fewer Birds to be heard, as fewer Trees for them to resort to. So I get to the Water: where Friends are not buried nor Pathways stopt up: but all is, as the Poets say, as Creation's Dawn beheld. I am happiest going in my little Boat round the Coast to Aldbro', with some Bottled Porter and some Bread and Cheese, and some good rough Soul who works the Boat and chews his Tobacco in peace.

In peace. He craved to be left in peace, yet also craved undemanding companionship. It was to Woodbridge that he brought Posh, the sailor he had met on Lowestoft beach, and it was here that he had his only other contact with his wife. To his amazement she appeared before him on the pavement one day when he was walking with the sailor, and held out her hand to him. FitzGerald automatically put out his hand, then snatched it back and hurried Posh on down the street.

He was becoming as eccentric and unpredictable as the eccentrics he had admired as a boy. How much of this was a pose and how much was his natural self it is difficult to decide. There is no doubt that he took a special delight in oddities of any kind. He collected local dialect expressions and nautical turns of phrase supplied by Posh. He became known as 'Old Fitz' to friends, neighbours, and townspeople of whose existence he was entirely unaware. His eyesight began to fail, he was even more easily exhausted than in his languid past, and after the death of one of his boatmen friends he even gave up his cherished boat. The Deben had lost its charm. For a while he contributed trite local notes to the *Ipswich Journal*, prepared as a loving duty his *Readings from Crabbe*, paid a last visit to Aldeburgh, and died in his sleep in June 1883. A plaque above the Woodbridge shop records his residence there. He is buried in Boulge churchyard, his grave marked by a rose bush nurtured from one upon the grave of Omar Khayyam.

A more sinister grave lies some way down Dobbs' Lane at Kes-

grave, off the main road between Woodbridge and Ipswich. Dobbs
was a shepherd who hanged himself in a barn in the eighteenth century and was buried in unhallowed ground at a crossroads on the
heath, now surrounded by bungalows. The poor wretch has since
been charitably supplied with concrete head and foot stones. Long
after his death there were those who doubted that 'Dobbs' Grave'
was a grave at all, or that any remains lay beneath the soil. After a
session at the 'Bell', a few worthies stiffened by alcohol reeled down
the road and dug up the grave. They found that there were indeed
human remains within. Before refilling the hole, one man wrenched
a tooth out of the jaw and is said to have worn it on his watch-chain
until the day he died.

Behind are the heaths of Martlesham, Brightwell and Foxhall. The
most tempting roads are those leading towards the western bank of
the Deben. At Waldringfield are more boats, tied up at buoys or
sprouting a plantation of tipsily divergent masts on the shore between sheds and summerhouses. Hemley, too, has its landing. Roads
down to the riverside now thin out, become lanes, become footpaths
—if you know where to look. Walk or sail: you see more, hear
more, and smell things other than tar, dust and gasoline.

Felixstowe Ferry is a Bohemian tangle of assorted shacks, holiday
bungalows, dinghies and oil drums looking across to Bawdsey Moor
and its infinitely more formal R.A.F. accommodation. The strip of
water known as King's Fleet reflects in spirit the royal convoy
assembled here in 1338 for the transport of troops to France and
the Battle of Crécy.

Strung along the shore towards the southern tip of this peninsula
is Felixstowe, the only truly wholehearted, frankly commercialized
seaside resort in Suffolk. In 90 years its population has increased ten-
fold: in 1880 it was a fishing community of about 2,000; today it
holds some 20,000.

That summing-up sounds pejorative. It is not meant to be so.
Felixstowe is as happy and bright as its name. Far down the coast
from Lowestoft, it is equally far in spirit. Brash, cheerful young
Felixstowe succeeds where soured Lowestoft, for all its admirable
history, fails.

There was a Roman station here, halfway between Landguard and Felixstowe Ferry. The Bigods later built one of their castles, but it fell victim to the sea and crumbled into ruin. In 1625 the building of Landguard Fort began on existing earthworks which had been strengthened at the time of the Armada to command the approaches to the Orwell and the Stour. In the early eighteenth century regular troops were withdrawn and replaced by an Invalid Company from Chelsea Hospital. In 1804 the Militia took over. Eight Martello towers were rushed up during the Napoleonic scare, two of which suffered the usual damage from coastal erosion and had to be demolished. The fort was rebuilt between 1871 and 1875, and became a saluting station. The last soldier left on 24 July 1957.

Felixstowe's rapid development as a watering place really began with the flurry of publicity surrounding a visit by the German Empress and her children in 1891. The promenade and sea wall were completed early in the new century, with a pier long enough to accommodate an electric tramway. Like so many others, the pier was chopped off during the last war. The railway brought profitable holiday traffic but has now been reduced to pay-train service and unstaffed halts. It seems absurd that as Felixstowe's busy docks expand to cope with the boom in container traffic, and the port sprawls out to face Parkeston Quay across the confluence of rivers, railway facilities decline while heavier and bulkier lorries make the roads more and more dangerous.

Factories and warehouses move out along a service road in the direction of Walton Ferry, obliterating the path which so recently led down from the 'Dooley'. It is to be hoped that future industrial developments will never debar picnickers from settling on the old fortifications, seamed by marks of guns from more modern conflicts, to watch Dutch and Danish ships and British Rail ferries move smoothly, purposefully in and out.

The name of the 'Dooley' inn is said by some to be a corruption of 'dole', a boundary pathway, and by others to come from the Indian 'Douali Tap'. Once upon a time, under a different name, it was a smugglers' haunt. The numerous doors to each room, inexplicable in contemporary terms and unrelated to the practical running of a pub, were there to foil both Preventive men and the press gangs.

Out through Trimley St Mary and Trimley St Martin the road to Ipswich is uninterruptedly busy, but a diversion towards the Orwell meanders along gentle slopes which have produced more than their fair crop of great seamen. Above Trimley Marshes, Grimston Hall was the home of Thomas Cavendish, the second Englishman to sail round the world. He returned a month after the defeat of the Armada, and as he sailed up the Thames past Greenwich Palace the Queen graciously waved to him. The information he brought back from his circumnavigation, added to that amassed by Hakluyt from his many informants, was influential in encouraging London merchants to equip expeditions to India and the Spice Islands—a far cry from gentle Trimley or Wetheringsett.

The 'Ship' inn at Levington may seem out of keeping in its rural surroundings, but many of its beams are fashioned from ships' timbers, and the smugglers' creek associated with Margaret Catchpole is no more than half a mile away. In the old days it was customary to trumpet a blast on the coach-horn as the conveyance rounded the sharp corner below and began the short, steep ascent to the inn—'Though who he thought he were goin' to knock over ...' says the present landlord with an expressive shrug. On the other side of the lonely road stands Hill Cottage, once belonging to the Broke family. Broke Hall, overlooking the Orwell between Levington and Nacton, was the birthplace of Philip Bowes Vere Broke. Commanding the frigate *Shannon* on patrol in the seas off Boston in 1813, he challenged the United States frigate *Chesapeake* to come out and fight. Within 15 minutes of opening fire the two ships were locked together, Broke led a boarding party, and the *Chesapeake* was captured. He was made a baronet, but the severe wounds sustained during the encounter forced him into retirement.

Neighbouring Orwell Park, an eighteenth-century building added to in a variety of styles during the nineteenth century, is now a school. It was the home of another, earlier, equally distinguished sailor, Admiral Vernon, known to his men as 'Old Grog' because, with the tenacity of some modern householder reluctant to part with a favourite pair of decrepit slippers, he clung to an old grogram cloak which he unfailingly wore on the quarter-deck. The nickname 'grog' was transferred, perhaps none too approvingly, to his issue of rum diluted with water in place of the neat spirit to which sailors had become accustomed.

Vernon was widely acclaimed as the victor of Porto Bello because of his capture of the town in 1739 with six ships and little loss of English life. As Porto Bello was defenceless at the time, this was hardly an outstanding achievement, but it made him popular with the public and gave him the strength to pursue his favourite occupation of writing vituperative letters and pamphlets concerning the innumerable follies of the Admiralty until, having nagged and excoriated his superiors beyond endurance, he was cashiered. He was M.P. for Ipswich for 16 years before his death. Both he and Broke are buried in Nacton church.

The true patron ghost of these shores, however, is Margaret Catchpole. Although much romanticized in the novel taking its title from her, she was a real person of whom there are some genuine and pathetic records. She appears to have been a tomboy, keen on riding, restless and eager for liberation from her drably unadventurous life as a servant. While in the employ of John Cobbold, the Ipswich brewer, she fell in love with William Laud, a young ferryman. Tempted to do a little smuggling, he became more deeply enmeshed than he had intended, and involved Margaret in his escapades around Ipswich, Bawdsey, Levington and Woolverstone. In the Window of Cat House, which to this day overlooks the Orwell from the grounds of Woolverstone Hall, a stuffed white cat was set as an 'all clear' sign to Laud and his associates.

In 1797 Margaret stole a coach horse belonging to the Cobbolds and rode to London, dressed as a young man. She aroused suspicion when trying to sell the horse, was arrested and returned to Ipswich, and found herself in Ipswich gaol. She escaped, and tried with Laud to get away to Holland via Orford. A local man informed on them, Laud was shot, and Margaret was recaptured and sentenced to transportation to Australia.

Richard Cobbold, whose father was able to give his two youngest sons a University education and to buy for each of them a church sinecure at £1,000 a year, no small income in the early nineteenth century, drew on family records and reminiscences when writing the novel. There is also a painting by him of Margaret Catchpole in Christchurch Mansion in Ipswich, and a stuffed lyrebird which she is reputed to have sent home from her Australian banishment.

An entry in the register of St Peter's, Richmond, New South Wales, reads:

Margaret Catchpole, aged 58 years, came prisoner in the 'Nile' in the year 1801, was buried May 14th, 1819.

There are some obvious discrepancies here. The dashing girl in the novel has aged with unreasonable speed! Whatever the sordid truth may have been, most of us will go on thinking of Margaret as Cobbold depicted her.

During our perambulation of the county we have once or twice lunged towards Ipswich and then veered away from it. Now it lies full across our route. The airport runway is close to the road. Suburbs encroach on the fields.

To get a good first impression of the town it might be wise to tackle the bewildering one-way system with but one aim in view—that of reaching Christchurch Mansion undeterred by any distraction on either side. This is close to the main shopping centre and to adequate car parks; though if you fail to espy the entrance to such parking spaces in good time and so overshoot, you will be committed to negotiating a large part of the circuit once more.

Christchurch Mansion preserves the best that Ipswich has to offer. At the town end of a spacious park, its lake stocked with many species of wildfowl, the house is a generously proportioned Elizabethan building to which additions were made in the seventeenth century after much of the roof and interior were burnt out. It was sold in 1732 to a Huguenot refugee, Claude Fonnereau, after whom one of the roads skirting the park is named. At the end of the last century there was a threat to pull it down to make way for modern housing, but Felix Cobbold came to the rescue, bought it, and presented it to the town, also leaving a large endowment in his will.

Today it houses a domestic museum complementing the natural history and archaeological collections in the High Street museum. Part of a sixteenth-century timber-framed house from Major's Corner was attached as an additional wing in 1924, and in 1931 a picture gallery was added to commemorate the four-hundredth anniversary of Cardinal Wolsey's death. Here are some Gainsborough paintings of the Orwell, and along many of the corridors are prints and paintings of the town at various periods of its history, most of them considerably more appealing than our contemporary streets and buildings.

Settlement of Ipswich does not seem to have been very vigorous in ancient times, though there are some scattered souvenirs of early residents. Five gold torcs from the first century B.C. were found in 1968 during building operations, declared treasure trove, and acquired by the British Museum. They were all unfinished, and in all probability had to be hurriedly concealed by the goldsmith in an emergency, perhaps as robbers raided his workshop. There was a Roman villa to the north, and Saxon cooking pots were found on the site of Woolworth's, in the area which had been the potters' quarter in Saxon times.

In the Middle Ages, Ipswich began to flourish as a port. King John granted the borough its first charter, and a seal was issued, depicting a small merchant ship of the day. The Orwell was a broad thoroughfare for the import of salt, wine, and building stone, and the Gipping may have been navigable as far as Rattlesden; certainly there was steady traffic up to Stowmarket after canalization in 1793.

Wolsey was born here, somewhere around 1475, the son of a grazier. It is suggested that Wolsey Bridge over the creek and marshland on the way into Reydon and Southwold is so called because he once drove his father's cattle over it to the slaughterhouse. He rose to become Archbishop of York and then a Cardinal. Having mishandled the problem of Henry VIII's divorce from Catherine of Aragon, he was brought down, and his cherished project for a great college in Ipswich crumbled in ruins with him. There remains only a gateway in College Street, overshadowed by dockland warehouses and factories, carrying on its arch the arms of Henry VIII, as worn and disfigured as though Dowsing himself had been at them.

David Garrick began his career here but had to leave to win fame. Gainsborough came here from Sudbury but was persuaded by his patron Phillip Thicknesse, governor of Landguard Fort, that he would win swifter recognition in the salons of Bath.

When the market for Suffolk cloth declined, Ipswich declined. The town was in the doldrums during the Georgian period and so lacks the staunch Georgian bone structure of so many Suffolk towns. It survived as a milling and malting centre, and as a garrison town and food distribution port during the Napoleonic wars. Road traffic began to steal trade from the rivers. Prosperity did not really begin to creep back until Robert Ransome set himself up here as a manufacturer of agricultural implements. The population trebled between 1801 and 1861. This expansion into the Victorian era brought the inevitable rash of undistinguished houses, shops, factories and civic buildings in between, around and over what good features remained.

Hemmed in by just such a jumble of nonentities, the Ancient House in Butter Market retains its exuberance. If its fate is to be that of a shop, competing in the modern shopping streets, at least let us be thankful that it is a bookshop and a good one at that. It is a brick and timber building of Elizabethan origin, resolved into its present form in 1957. It has attractively gabled windows in the roof, leaded oriel windows along the first floor, and the most ambitious pargeting in the county, some of it in such heavy relief that it deserves rather to be called sculpture. Between the ground-floor and first-floor windows are designs symbolic of the continents then known—that is, minus Australasia. A whole section of the west wall represents Atlas supporting his globe and accepting the respects of a shepherd and a flock of sheep, recalling the days of wool exporting. Inside, the ceilings are richly ornamented, some in plaster and some with carved beams. Tradition has it that the oldest part of the building, a tiny chapel concealed in the roof and forgotten until 1801, was Charles II's bolt-hole after the battle of Worcester. From some time in the latter part of the sixteenth century until the middle of the nineteenth century the house was in the hands of one family, the Sparrowes, and is still often referred to as Sparrowe's House.

In Tavern Street is the 'Great White Horse', where a certain young reporter from the *Morning Chronicle* twice stayed when visiting the town to describe election campaigns. A little while later he wrote *Pickwick Papers*, in which he had such unpleasant things to say about the hotel that the landlord threatened a libel action.

'The Great White Horse' is famous in the neighbourhood, in the same degree as a prize ox, or county-paper chronicled turnip, or unwieldy pig—for its enormous size. Never were such labyrinths ...such huge numbers of small dens for eating or sleeping in ...

Charles Dickens nevertheless seemed to like the town itself, for he chose to return for the last of his famous public readings on 31 October 1861.

In 1966 the owners wished to pull the hotel down and build a shop and office block. Denied Corporation permission, they appealed, but after a public enquiry the Minister of Housing upheld the ban.

In company with Hadleigh, Ipswich was designated an 'overspill' area for London, with estimated increase in population of 60,000 by 1981. This proposal seems to have been abandoned for the time being. 'Overspill' is in any case an ugly word for an unpleasant concept: it conjures up all too accurately a vision of a glutton so incapable of restraint that food begins to dribble down its chin, tie and lapels. Suffolk can well do without the products of London's incontinence.

The A.138 escapes with commendable speed from Ipswich into the last of the county's shallow peninsulas. The road follows the Orwell for a brief spell: with Ipswich behind one, there is nothing to mar the sheen on the river or the green quietude of the near and far banks. Even the cargo boats ripple rather than clank past. All too soon the road curls inland towards Freston.

Between road and river, Freston Tower thrusts up like some abandoned steeple with an improbable complement of windows. This Elizabethan folly, with its six rooms stacked one above another, may have been built simply on a whim, or could have belonged to a merchant impatiently watching for the return of his argosy.

It is easy to drive on through Chelmondiston without paying too much attention to the village. St Andrew's church is post-war, replacing one bombed by the Luftwaffe, and looks drab and unimaginative from outside. Inside its colour washes and generous windows produce an appealing brightness quite at odds with that grey exterior. There is an old hour-glass by the pulpit, presumably for decorative purposes only.

Hidden away at the end of the precipitous, narrow lane which curves past the church is a boat hard, one of the major visual delights on the Orwell. Here at Pinmill are laid up brown-sailed barges which once did a busy trade between these coasts and the wharves of London, and whose annual race was a great event. The mud and water, the barges and dinghies and craft of every kind, are overlooked by the side windows of the old 'Butt and Oyster', which can surely boast the best prospect of any tavern in the land. Its bar provided the background for a familiar old tobacco advertisement, a copy of which, much darkened by time and nicotine, still hangs on the wall. Pinmill's name is said to result from a local landowner's gift to his daughter: she was given the profits from windmills on his land as pin money. It sounds too charming to be true, but we may choose to enjoy the charm rather than accept the cold reality.

The main road, which we rejoin up another narrow one-way lane, stops at the edge of the Stour where Shotley Gate looks across the haven to Harwich. The wooden-walled *Ganges* has given its name to an area of shore which has itself come to resemble a ship, bright with masts and flags. The tip of the promontory is best seen from the water—from the Harwich ferry or from one of the ships heading out towards Europe. Many a voyager who has never set foot in Suffolk will have enjoyed the slow turn below Shotley, out beyond Landguard Point, until the whole bright arc of Felixstowe's cheerful waterfront reveals itself.

Heading seaward or landward, we are about to run out of Suffolk. Essex lies there on the far side of the Stour; and if we take the roads along the southern rim of this peninsula, we shall find Essex waiting there too.

CHAPTER EIGHT

Exit

I wonder how many things will have changed during even the short time this book is with the printers? And if it is taken off a library shelf ten years from now, how misleading will it be, how far out of date? 'Time don' 'arf fly—that's a 'ell of a job to keep up wi'', as I've heard it said in slow Suffolk sing-song.

The Romans left, Christians backed away from the Angles, the Danes came and went. American airmen were glad to turn their backs on the windswept airfields when the war ended, and those who do a tour of duty on the present airfields are probably equally relieved when the time comes to go home. Or are they? Remembering John Appleby and his *Suffolk Summer*, one can't be too sure.

Modern visitors, fortunate in being able to choose their own time and their own itinerary, carry what impressions with them when they leave? Some hazy, some firmly fixed, no doubt; some opinions as dogmatic as those of the locals who want no change in what they have known, or who claim resentfully that there has already been irremediable change.

We have seen the appeal boards outside crumbling churches, the notices advertising traction engine rallies, bazaars, and gardens open to the public—some for this charity or that restoration fund, some simply to help in the upkeep of the houses whose loss would affect not merely their owners but the whole community. Old inns have been modernized, old farmhouses converted into private dwellings for retired Army officers, stockbrokers, merchants, pig breeders, and for those writers and painters who can afford to maintain them. Lead-sheathed electricity cables and wire are stapled to blackened, pitted beams and led in twisted patterns down walls, across ceilings and over chimney breasts. Old sculleries rumble to the throb of central heating furnaces, and no longer need the services of the 'back'us' boy.

It would be difficult to find a boy nowadays prepared to do all the drudgery behind the scenes from dawn to dusk, with quite a lot of overlap at either end. In the backhouse of farm or inn there would, in the old days, be the oven, the copper, perhaps the pump, and all the equipment for cooking, pickling and brewing. An old story is told of the back'us boy who complained, in those times when there were no regulations concerning hours and terms of employment, 'I reck'n thass a roight owl life, that is—wark all noight fer one an' six a day an' then yew get nuffen ... I call *that* suffen!'

But the changes and conversions, losses and readjustments, have not been too great and have not all been bad. Suffolk's coastline may be soft and easily demolished, but its people are tough and shrewd when it comes to deciding whether to repel invaders or cunningly to assimilate them.

I have included no formal list of acknowledgments in these pages because any such list would either be too long or would have to omit names of people who have done so much to help. Similarly I am giving no source books: like friends, acquaintances and courteous strangers, there have been so many of them, and I am grateful not so much for specific facts gleaned from them as for the sparks struck, the stimulus to go and see for myself, the nudge towards something I might otherwise have missed.

Perhaps the traveller leaving Suffolk will be haunted by certain memories and want to retain some contact. He will find that plenty has been written in and about Suffolk. The county has also provided strength to many writers who have not specifically used it as a theme for their works. Rider Haggard spent some time at Cliff Grange, Kessingland. Eric Blair lived for a while in Southwold and included a Suffolk river in his pseudonym of George Orwell. A member of the Critten family of Southwold wrote as Neil Bell and as Stephen Southwold. We have already paid our respects to Hakluyt, Crabbe, Borrow and FitzGerald, and to ardent visitors such as Dickens; and we might add Sir John Suckling from the family associated for centuries with Barsham, and John Lydgate, the poet monk of Lidgate. H. W. Freeman's *Joseph and his Brethren* grew in Badingham. More recently Adrian Bell and George Ewart Evans have left an indelible mark.

If I am to risk naming any contemporary books, I think I must select Norman Scarfe's *Suffolk—a Shell Guide* as a portable, know-ledgeable, crisply and often wittily informative reference book; and as a lyrical work which, though dealing only with one small parish, miraculously evokes the whole county past and present, there is Ronald Blythe's *Akenfield*.

So we are on our way towards the gate by which we came in. Time for a last meal, a last snack on Suffolk soil before leaving? Unfortunately, as a writer in the *East Anglian Magazine* observed not so long ago, 'The standard of mediocrity in most of the restaur-ants of the area is truly impressive.' Devotees of the good ones are selfishly reluctant to publicize them.

It is odd that, in spite of intensive dairy farming in many parts of the county, no distinctive marketable cheese has ever been produced to compete with those of Cheshire, Wensleydale, Caerphilly, Glou-cester or other localities. I have never been offered a Suffolk cheese or come across one in any shop or market. Older friends assure me I have missed nothing. In the days when one such was commonly made, it proved so markedly individual that generations later than that of Robert Bloomfield have preferred to forget it. Bloomfield was blunt:

Unrivalled stands thy country CHEESE, O Giles!
Whose very name alone engenders smiles.
Its name derision and reproach pursue,
And strangers tell of 'three times skimmed sky blue'
To cheese converted; what can be its boast?
What but the common virtues of a post.
If drought o'ertake it faster than the knife,
Most fair it bids for stubborn length of life,
And like the oaken shelf whereon 'tis laid,
Mocks the weak efforts of the bending blade;

Or in the hog trough rests in perfect spite,
Too big to swallow and too hard to bite.

No restaurant lunch, then; and no bread and cheese in the village inn. On from Shotley along the road which runs above the estuary, offering glimpses of water between the rising and falling waves of farmland. A tight bend to the left unexpectedly reveals the brick lodge gateway of Erwarton Hall, pinnacled as though with the chimneys of some inexplicable subterranean furnace. Approaching Harkstead we get varying angles on the soaring clock-tower of the Royal Hospital School at Holbrook, and soon pass between nicely regimented housing and the entrance gates. The school, for the sons of officers and men in the Royal Navy and Royal Marines, was transferred here from Greenwich in 1933.

Half a mile to the north, most easily reached by a footpath from Stutton, is Alton Mill. This has stood upon its stream for about 200 years, replacing earlier watermills which are known to have occupied the site since before Domesday. The wheel and mechanism worked until 1947. The mill is scheduled as an Ancient Monument but is nevertheless in danger: there have for some time been proposals to make a reservoir, under whose surface this and much of the gentle, secretive little vale may disappear.

The road between Stutton and Tattingstone passes a remarkable structure known with some justice as the Tattingstone Wonder. What looks from a distance like a stunted church tower trapped in the gable of a farmhouse turns out to be a freakish clump of cottages decked out as a make-believe church—an eighteenth-century bourgeois folly.

We can pick up the A.137 from Ipswich just outside Brantham and follow its convergence upon the railway line which runs on a low bridge across Cattawade Creek, dominated by the Xylonite works, towards London. But we started in Constable country, and may most appropriately end in it by turning off through East Bergholt.

Here the painter was born in 1776. Within the church is a memorial to his wife, Maria; in a corner of the churchyard his father and mother are buried.

The church, like its surrounding village, was one of Constable's earliest subjects, and he returned to it many times. Basically a Tudor structure, it has only the unfinished stump of a tower, supposedly abandoned at the time of Wolsey's fall from grace: strange that no subsequent benefactor should have come to its rescue in such an affluent community. The bells are hung upside down in a wooden cage in the churchyard, and are rung by hand on the wooden headstocks.

Inside the church, the puce and green glass in the upper windows produces on a sunny day an effect as horrible as light through lurid lollipops. The gaily painted organ, on the other hand, is charming. There are some good monuments, and in the south chapel a nice limed oak screen. The centre window of the south aisle, dedicated to John Constable, incorporates his own sketch of the chancel and sanctuary, and Willy Lott's immortal cottage.

Edwarde Lamb won himself a desirable epitaph:

With his Councell he helped many: yett
took fees scarsse of Any.
Died Nov. 1617.

It is more soothing than that of John Mattinson, who, the terror and delight of his pupils, was 'eleven years the beloved schoolmaster of this Town, and then unfortunately shott'. One would love to know the circumstances of this accident ... or assassination.

Willy Lott lies in the churchyard. As we observed on our way in, his cottage, which in 80 years he never left for more than four days in succession, stands where it always stood. Constable's family home is no more.

The late Randolph Churchill lived here. His old home has provided the basis for a landscaped Garden Centre, open to the public, with five acres of woodland and water gardens, shrubs, bulbs, roses, conifers and other trees.

Paul Jennings, who settled in this village some years ago, revealed in his contribution to *A Suffolk Garland for the Queen* when Queen Elizabeth II toured the county, that he was born in Warwickshire: 'But I would like to die in Suffolk. Not yet, of course'.

I would like to match that with a neat phrase of my own but have decided not to try. I will simply echo it, and wave the visitor sorrowfully in the direction of the main road and on down to London (since for us roads and railways into London are 'down' rather than 'up'). For myself, I turn back towards the coast.

At the parting of the ways we are in the region nowadays known so mellifluously as IP9. Wending a homeward path around the creeks and inlets, through the forests and over the heath to the ship-surge of the church in IP17 and the bird-flickering mudflats beyond, I make a brief ascent to the turn-off and am on the last lap into bleak, warm, sunny, misty, infuriating, loving and lovable IP18-6LP, a name which will surely strike a chord in the heart of anyone who has ever known and adored Suffolk.

Just over a week ago we were listening to a recital of salty Northumbrian songs in Aldeburgh. The laburnum was paling and ready to fall. Two evenings ago a sky of pink-streamered ultramarine glowed above Snape and above Mozart's *Idomeneo*. Our son has been across the road, down the steps and into the sea most afternoons on his return home from school. Only last night, not so many hours before typing these final paragraphs, I was in a garden at Henham, the air still, the glass of wine cool, as the Lantern Singers concluded their programme on the lawn with two unforgettable Suffolk songs—*The Foggy Foggy Dew* and *The Ladybird*. The Henham rhododendrons are past their peak, but the rhododendron maze will be heavy with bloom again next year. Sea winds have failed to destroy the roses. There is clematis everywhere. Hedgerows and banks and the seafront cliff walks of Southwold are a scarlet dazzle of poppies. People sit outside the 'Red Lion' on South Green, narrowing their eyes blissfully against the brightness. The locals slow their pace, stop and talk: 'Looks as though we're in for a good summer.' A dour, sceptical, yet not altogether pessimistic nod of the head: 'That need.'

It will always be here, all of it, the music and the flowers, sea and bright sky and timber and plaster and unconquerable flint, for anyone who cares to come back.

Most people do come back.

Index

Index

Index